Discover Laws of the Universe:

Your Guide to Personal and Spiritual Transformation

By

Dr. Bruce A. Johnson

Copyright 2018 Dr. Bruce A. Johnson

All rights reserved.

Table of Contents

Introduction 1

CHAPTER 1. ONE MAN'S TRANSFORMATIONAL JOURNEY   7

   Discovering Self-Acceptance 12

   Why Would Someone Choose to Live a Unique Life? 18

CHAPTER 2. EVERYTHING IS ENERGY 25

   What is Energy? 26

   What is the Mind and Body Connection? 29

   What Are Names Associated with Energy? 32

   Is Energy the Same as God or a Supreme Being? 36

   What Are the Different Forms of Energy? 46

   Lessons Learned 47

CHAPTER 3. COLLECTIVE CONSCIOUSNESS 49

   The Energy Source of Life 50

   Our Connection to Collective Consciousness 52

   Live Your Current Reality 57

CHAPTER 4. LAWS OF THE UNIVERSE 67

   Law of Connection: Forming Attachments 69

   Law of Attunement: Changing Your Focus and Vibration 74

   Law of Interaction: Internal and External Interactions 78

   Law of Intention: Creating Your Own Life 82

   Law of Clarity: Understanding the Purpose of Challenges 86

   Law of Presence: Fulfilling Your Purpose 91

   The Law of the Duality of Energy: Experiencing Negative Emotions 98

   Self-Reflection Worksheet: 106

CHAPTER 5. THE IMPORTANCE OF YOUR MINDSET **107**
   How to Tap into and Benefit from Universal Wisdom............ 110
   How Do You Find Answers to Important Questions?............... 115
   Understand the Energy of Change.. 119
   How to Find Relief from Feeling Overwhelmed 124
   What Is the Higher Purpose of Gratitude? 128
   How Do You Keep a Positive Outlook About Life?.................... 134

CHAPTER 6. READ AND BELIEVE **141**
   How Do You Learn Self-Worth?... 142
   How Do You Find Abundance?... 148
   Can Someone Amend Their Life's Plan?.. 153
   What are Random Events?... 160
   Who Is Controlling the Universe? 166

CHAPTER 7. HOW TO GUIDE **171**
   Discover How to Bring About Your Transformation................ 171

About the Author

Dr. Bruce A. Johnson is an inspirational author, writer, and teacher. His advanced education, background, experience, and training are within the field of adult education and distance learning. Dr. J now shares his most important work with his unique ability to gain insight and wisdom as a teacher of Laws of the Universe.

Introduction

I imagine you and I meeting for the first time and what I would share with you. What I would want to tell you about is what I have learned, as a means of helping to guide you and provide insight for the future ahead of you. More importantly, I would want to instill within you a sense of hope.

I want you to know you are not controlled. You do not need to live in fear of eternal damnation. You do not need to pray, beg, plead, or appease a supreme being to live your life. You do not need someone to act on your behalf in order to gain the knowledge and wisdom needed to live your life. You have access to this wisdom and it is available through your mind.

Your future is yours to create, just as you have already planned. Someone or something else is not dictating your life. *Your future is now.*

Instead of spending your life visualizing a new future, *live your life now*. You are meant to experience your life exactly as it is now. So much unhappiness comes from thinking you can visualize tomorrow and it is impossible to know the specifics of what tomorrow may bring when you have yet to create it.

Humans have been taught the concept of control but you do not have to be controlled. You can be free to live and create your own life. *There is hope for your future.*

Even though you control your own life, you do not need to be afraid as there is still order in the universe. But the universe is not the source of control. The source of life energy sustains every living thing and within this living energy is the Collective Consciousness of mankind, and from this energy source comes physical human forms who in turn nurture the source of life energy. It is a perpetual or never-ending cycle.

My name is Dr. Bruce A. Johnson.

I am an inspirational author, writer, and teacher. My background, experience, and training are in the field of adult learning. I am now sharing my most important work, with a unique ability to gain insight and wisdom as a teacher of Laws of the Universe.

I have a highly practiced ability, not a special gift or power, to be able to listen and connect to the Collective Consciousness and higher order Universal Wisdom of mankind. Throughout my life I have found myself not fitting into any traditional description and this has made me introspective and reflective, which has helped me learn to listen to and receive greater wisdom, insight, and knowledge.

My personal philosophy about being a teacher of the Laws of the Universe is this: I am a seeker of knowledge. I want to learn so that I can in turn help myself and teach others.

While I am in a reflective state of focused thinking, I am not assessing the knowledge and insight gained from a perspective of being "right" or "wrong" - it is a matter of what could be described as knowing. I am also not aware of a particular person or persons either. I am not attempting to contact anyone. I am connecting to a body of knowledge which comes from a collective repository of mankind. More importantly, someone is not speaking to me or through me. I have a question I use as a starting point and I am able to access a virtual repository of knowledge, through energetic impulses.

<u>A Point of Reference</u>: Some people have asked what my point of reference is while I am asking questions during my focused thinking.

As a traditional teacher, I would utilize a course textbook, along with my experience and knowledge of the subject. A motivational speaker might use what they have studied or learned. A preacher will base a sermon upon a sacred text and other foundational doctrines established by the institution. A popular Law of Attraction teacher conducts all live seminars with a mock connection to what is called "source" through channeling.

However, I find this interesting as I am not aware of energy being able to speak. Imagine placing your finger in an outlet and stating it is going to channel or speak through you. It usually does not work this way.

My point of reference is what I have learned while I am connected to the Collective Consciousness and higher order Universal Wisdom. I do not have a religious affiliation, I have rejected religious dogma long ago, and I find the current emphasis on Law of Attraction by New Age teachers to be inadequate for helping to address those who need guidance and are seeking answers about Laws of the Universe.

Learn About My Background

Throughout my life I have always been intuitive, and had an ability to sense and feel very strongly, although I have not always been willing to accept the nature of who I am. I tried to be "normal" for a quite a long time. It took time to recover from that disposition and sense of dislike about myself. I was also raised in a very strict, religious environment as a young person, which meant I was taught I was supposed believe a certain way about the order of the universe.

As an adult I abandoned all of those beliefs and held no religious viewpoint, rejecting the dogma being taught by most churches as it did not agree with what I felt inside. Later in life, I searched for answers as I had a growing list of questions I could not find answers to, as I wanted to know more about the world around me.

Approximately nine years ago, I came across *The Secret* and this is when I was first introduced to Law of Attraction. I read books and online articles published by many of the teachers from this book, including the teacher whose work it is based upon but is not featured within the book, Esther Hicks.

As I conducted further research into the Law of Attraction, I was surprised to find this idea has been around since the early 1900s. At that time, it was part of the New Thought Movement.

In 1900 William Walter Atkinson wrote: *"Anything is yours, if you only want it hard enough. Just think of it. ANYTHING. Try it. Try it in earnest and you will succeed. It is the operation of a mighty Law."* The New Thought Movement continued in its popularity until the 1960s.

The interest in Law of Attraction was not as prominent again until *The Secret* came out in 2009, although Esther Hicks had begun her teachings about Law of Attraction in the 1980s. This book made it seem as if answers to life could be easily attained through Law of Attraction.

There has been a great deal written about the Law of Attraction, especially within spiritual, self-help, and self-development articles, blog posts, and books. But it was *The Secret* which launched Law of Attraction into the spotlight. The "secret" had to do with a person's ability to focus on whatever they desire, and through the power of their focus and visualization or imagery of what was to be manifested, it would become possible to attract what was wanted into their life. It seemed like a simple concept to understand and apply, and if it could produce results that easily, it was understandable why many people were drawn to it.

I studied the teachers who were included in the video, which was produced in conjunction with the book. The use of Law of Attraction seemed to be the easiest answer for these teachers to offer, when answering most of the questions people were asking about their lives. I also observed those who sought out the teachings of Law of Attraction did not ask questions which went beyond the usual topics of relationships, finances, and careers.

In reality, this principle of Law of Attraction is true. If someone truly could focus that well and make a conscious change, their results would improve dramatically. But most people hear about Law of Attraction, try it, and cannot sustain it, and they go back to their teachers again - with the same questions about the same topics.

While I did find it was helpful to learn about Law of Attraction, and the teachers of Law of Attraction for my transformation, I also knew there had to be more involved. I read many critiques of Law of Attraction, including people who felt frustrated by the lack of changes in their lives as a result of their visualized wishes.

This is when I began to learn to concentrate and focus my thinking. I learned this through my work as an author and writer, by tapping into a consciousness stream and finding an infinite source of ideas and thoughts. I eventually realized I was tapping into a source of wisdom, which is the Collective Consciousness of mankind. I began to realize the source of life is energy and by knowing this my mind and entire world opened up.

Why I Became a Teacher of Laws of the Universe

A great teacher is not born from a life of ease and no experience. A teacher emerges from a well-worn path, with a mental suitcase full of experiences and memories, along with challenges and problems that have tested the very limits of this person's endurance. This person is someone who can empathize with others and has great words to inspire others with. *Greater teachers are later teachers.*

I decided to live a unique life, not fit in, not be normal according to societal terms, and defy the rules of society and religion. It would be a life filled with planned challenges, experiences, great highs, deep lows, loves that seemed to come and go, until a day later in life it would all lead to this new career path.

I am attuned to Collective Consciousness as is all of mankind, but I have gone further and attuned to Universal Wisdom. I did this by removing bias, religious perspectives, fear of punishment, and being able to trust what I am receiving when I attune. I simply focus like a radio changing stations to pick up another frequency. You do not see those frequencies in the air, rather you experience them with your senses.

When I attune, I have a point of reference or a question. Then as I accesses Universal Wisdom, it is like a vast library where I am reading from a book and this is the block of thought I am receiving as I write and take notes. When I am seeking an answer to a question, it is also like making a query in a database of knowledge.

I do not claim to have special powers, abilities, or answers to all of your questions. What I have is an ability to be quiet and listen to a Collective Consciousness, which has been called Infinite Intelligence or Source Energy by many, and this is something anyone can train themselves to do with time and practice.

Learning truths about the essence of our being and the source of life has been a transformational experience as I have come to know life from a completely new perspective. Now I want to share with you what I have learned in my journey, which is still ongoing. I believe there are others like myself who have questions which Law of Attraction, and teachers of Law of Attraction, cannot fully answer. Once you have discovered the many Laws of the Universe, and the universal truths, perhaps you will begin your own transformational journey of discovery and personal awakening.

I hope you are inspired by what you read.

Dr. Bruce A. Johnson
2018

CHAPTER 1.
ONE MAN'S TRANSFORMATIONAL JOURNEY

Becoming a teacher of Laws of the Universe was not something I intentionally set out to do until recently, after I discovered there was something meaningful I could tap into and share with others. This has been an evolutionary journey, with some elements of my journey known early on in life, and others learned through time and experience. As a child, the only clue I had about where my life would be at today was a desire to teach others - even when I could not understand what it was I was doing. As you read about my transformational journey you will discover my love of teaching was a common thread throughout all of my experiences.

What you will also find, as you read through the phases of my transformational journey, is that I have always felt a natural sense of being pulled towards something - though it appeared to be extreme unhappiness for most of my life. It wasn't until now, at a later point in my life, when I can see my past experiences as lessons learned. There has been nothing about my life which has been easy or stress free. I wasn't born with a silver spoon in my mouth, I struggled to make ends meet, and there have been health challenges along the way. Despite all of the problems and issues, I learned to listen and trust the guidance within me, refusing to give up.

Something else which made my life unique was never accepting the religious teachings I heard. While I was adversely impacted by the negative and abusive language experienced at a young and impressionable age, it did not mean I believed it. Yet I heard it, I felt it, and I wasn't supported in my feelings of being different. The result was hiding my true identity for many years.

Now I realize this was all part of the lessons I needed to learn, so I could help empower and inspire others who may also have had this experience. Even after I discovered Law of Attraction, I could instinctually sense there was still more to life than what was being taught, and this is what led me to become a teacher of Laws of the Universe.

Phase One: Childhood Memories

I grew up in a blue collar, middle-class family, with of my both parents working full time jobs. My father was a police officer and I remember how caring and compassionate he was, and how he taught his sons the value of hard work. This work ethic is something which has stayed with me to this very day. Watching my mother work and raise three children also inspired me as well, as she was another source of unending strength.

One of the most important memories I had as a child, looking back now on my life, was a budding love of teaching. I remember going to garage sales and buying textbooks I could not fully comprehend, pretending I was teaching students about subjects I did not understand. The other significant event in my childhood was the introduction of religious extremism. At some point as a young person my parents joined an evangelical church. This introduced very strong, negative rhetoric into our family, along with condemnation about any characteristic or lifestyle which did not meet the strict definition prescribed by the church.

While I did not embrace the dogma or rhetoric I heard, it did instill within me a deep sense of loathing because of the internal conflict I was already experiencing. I was feeling something about my true self which I could not understand and it was at a time in society when there were no visible gay characters on television or in the movies, there were few resources available, and the Internet had not yet arrived. I also had no one I felt I could talk to as these feelings had isolated me at school and caused me to become an outsider. The only escape I could find was part time employment outside of the house, which allowed me to eventually make a few friends. Once I graduated from high school, the only option I believed I had was to escape through a traditional marriage.

Phase Two: Life as a Young Adult

The next phase of my life was not any easier from a personal perspective as I was still hiding my true self and feeling internal conflict. From a professional perspective, my career was progressing though for many years it was in an industry I did not intend to work in. Although I wasn't in a teaching career yet, and I had not consciously considered it, I held jobs which allowed me to help others. I found opportunities to teach training classes, regardless of my job title or position, which was a fit for my natural interests. But it was challenging to think about developing my career when the internal conflict about my identity was becoming so intense. Finally, I made a decision to make a significant lifestyle change.

Phase Three: A Time of Change

I initiated the next phase of my life, which involved getting a divorce and coming out. I knew it was time to live my truth and put an end to the internal conflict I was experiencing. To help me regain my focus I went back to school, earned my first master's degree, and made a transition into corporate training. Now I had initiated both personal and professional changes. However, this was not an easy time in my life as I entered a stage where I faced life from a new perspective. Even though I made these changes it did not mean I was prepared for a new life, especially after having lived with strong internal conflict for so many years.

Phase Four: Facing New Challenges

The internal conflict experienced for most of my life, combined with external pressures resulting from the transitory period I had initiated, culminated in a stress-related health condition. This was a debilitating condition which left me bedridden and forced to consider a career change. It was during this time period I had to fight to recover and cope with a condition which would not end any time soon. What I discovered while I was recovering was a lesson in living according to life's plan, as the next chapter in my career opened up. This was the time I began my career in distance learning, and it encouraged me to continue my education as a means of keeping myself focused and my mind strong.

While I was learning to adapt to my health condition, I was moving into a career which felt very natural to me, one which allowed me to teach, inspire, mentor, coach, and nurture the growth and development of others. I learned to connect with students, build from their strengths, and teach positivity. I learned to empathize with both the everyday or ordinary challenges, along with the extraordinary challenges which students can face while trying to better their lives. I also studied adult learning and chose a doctorate in adult education to gain as much knowledge as I could about the learning process. I quickly rose through the ranks and took on leadership roles, working with faculty and students in the same teaching, mentoring, and coaching capacity.

Phase Five: Discovering Law of Attraction

During the time of my recovery and career transition, there was an important discovery and it was finding the Law of Attraction. You will read about this in much more detail throughout the book; however, discovering the Law of Attraction helped prompt an awakening within me. For the first time in my life I found something that felt naturally right, as to how it aligned with the way I experienced it from within. This is in comparison to the natural misalignment I felt whenever I was in a church and heard religious dogma, and I could not accept what I heard as truth about life. I spent many years studying Law of Attraction and following the teachers of Law of Attraction. What I learned is that I have a natural ability to listen and more importantly, I could naturally attune to a Collective Consciousness while in a reflective state.

At first this ability to reflect and connect with a Collective Consciousness helped my work as an author and writer. I found my ability to write articles and blog posts about education and career topics became much more engaging and in-depth. I was connecting to a broader base of knowledge and I understood the limitless nature of the consciousness I could tap into. Then I began to realize I could attune further and receive greater wisdom, which lead me to realize I was attuning to Universal Wisdom. This helped lead me to the next phase in my life.

Phase Six: A Year of Awakening

By 2017 I was now an experienced educator, mentor, and coach. I was also a published author and writer. I was fully aware of my ability to attune to Collective Consciousness and higher order Universal Wisdom. I had been following one of the primary teachers of Law of Attraction but realizing that the use of channeling was just a technique to control the audience interaction. We are all part of the energy source of life. No one needs to wait for someone to channel a source to access this insight and wisdom.

In 2017 I finally heard this Law of Attraction teacher live during a cruise, and I was surprised to see many of the same people in attendance who had been in prior workshops over the past few years. The same questions from prior workshops were being asked, and the same answers were being given by this teacher. I realized this teacher could only give one set of answers as Law of Attraction is the basis of her platform - and this law has limitations as to what it can explain. I knew if more Laws of the Universe were being taught, there would be more answers provided, and these questions would not be asked repeatedly by her followers.

It was at this point and time I decided I needed to start to share what I was able to access. It was then I discovered this was part of the plan I had created for my life, to be a teacher of Laws of the Universe. This is when I set out to ask questions and gain new insight from the Collective Consciousness and higher order

Universal Wisdom, to help anyone who wants to learn about life and the source of life we are all connected to. My goal is to empower others to learn how to attune to the wisdom and insight all humans have access to at any given time. I am a teacher because I am practiced in attuning to this consciousness stream, and I have life experiences I can share to inspire as well.

Now consider what it means to live a unique life. I lived a unique life. If your life was out of the ordinary, or different in some way, you may find this next section to be inspiring.

Discovering Self-Acceptance

Are there aspects of your life which you cannot seem to control no matter how hard you try, no matter how much time and effort you devote to making changes?

Here are some examples: Do you struggle with trying to lose weight? Do you devote time to building muscle, improving your appearance, or changing how you look in some manner?

It seems we are constantly reminded about the need to be thinner, look more beautiful, increase our attractiveness or masculinity, and if we do so, our lives will somehow get better. There are endless advertisements on television, in online publications, and within print magazines as well, which show us there is an ideal image in our society which we should be all striving to achieve. This is designed by marketers to create a need within us to purchase whatever product is being advertised, to help us achieve the goal we all are trying to chase after, whether it is related to looks, wealth, or success.

For many people, this creates an internal sense of struggle and conflict. There may be an attempt to purchase and use the next magic supplement, diet plan, piece of workout equipment, or cookbook to some degree of success. But more often than not, most purchases seem to gather dust over time, when instantaneous results do not seem to happen. This only further amplifies the feeling of failure, especially if a person is not thin, or highly successful, or extremely wealthy, or all these factors combined.

It can be quite exhausting living in a society which is always sending out visual cues that remind us of who we are supposed to be, especially when there are just as many other visual cues seen on television, which tempt us with over-size food proportions to be found at our nearest fast food restaurants.

I have to admit I was on this roller coaster ride for quite a long time and yes, it all started or originated as a child. I was the fat kid who was teased mercilessly at school because he was overweight, liked to eat, and detested gym class or anything involving sports. It seemed I ran away from a chubby fat kid for many years. Occasionally I gave in and stated to myself, "who cares", only to gain a lot of weight and then feel guilt and shame. The lack of caring attitude did not solve my problem, and losing weight helped to regain a sense of control but it did not resolve the inner natural turmoil.

I have read many techniques about being body consciousness and how a person is supposed to recover from this state of mind. One method involves looking in the mirror and gradually accepting each part of your body, showing self-love for each area that you might deem to be a flaw or imperfection. This seemed to be okay, as long as you can look at yourself and not feel the internal sense of dislike.

What then caused a shift in my mindset? It was a matter of simply stating: This is me! That was as simple as it could be in terms of a solution. I finally just looked at myself without judgement or any emotion other than kindness and stated those three words. It was a simple act of self-acceptance, without attaching any conditions to it. I didn't state: This is me as long as I can accomplish something. The phrase was just: This is me!

Understanding self-acceptance from this perspective has taught me a great deal about myself and helping others. You just have to reach a point where you no longer want to put yourself down or wait for certain conditions to arrive before you can like or love yourself. This is when you can release negative energy and cause a shift in your thinking and how you feel about your life. It doesn't mean you no longer care about how you look or feel, but now you act from a new perspective, one that is out of love and care for yourself, rather than dislike, disgust, or internal conflict.

I realize now that self-acceptance is a powerful form of energy and I wanted to learn more as I was attuned to Collective Consciousness and higher order Universal Wisdom. I will share with you what I have learned about the energy of self-acceptance.

A universal truth is this: Look around at the life contained on this planet, other than the humans. How many varieties of plants can you identify? How many trees can you name? Do you know the name of every type of animal roaming across the lands? More importantly, do you think of these living beings as grotesque or in need of change in some manner? For trees and plants, humans marvel at the beauty as they explore new blooms or go out in nature and experience the vast growth of trees reaching far up into the sky. And when man experiences wildlife, it is often with a sense of awe and wonder, at the magnificence of such creatures and how they seem to survive on their own, out in what appears to be the wilds.

Yet these are all living, energetic beings. These beings are nurtured by the energy of life. While these living beings may not carry the memories that humans do, memories which go into the Collective Consciousness of mankind, these beings do in fact have a connection to the source of life energy. Through the operation by the Collective Consciousness, these beings are an intelligent energetic form of life. This allows these beings to grow, to be nurtured, to be sustained, or be neglected, and according to its design, eventually end a lifecycle.

These life forms serve a purpose, as do all living things. These living beings exist without judgement or negative energy. It is human beings who carry memories and contribute to the Collective Consciousness who are the ones existing with positive and negative energy, necessary to balance the energy source of life. And the negative energy can take on many forms within a human being.

The Bondage of Negativity

For many humans, negative energy is similar to putting on shackles, or self-imposed restraints. Humans, through generations of conditioning, find that focusing on negative elements or aspects of life is much easier to do. A person can trap themselves into a cycle of hurt, pain, and self-doubt for so long they never know any other life but a negative one. This prevents them from ever truly breaking free unless they can learn to tear down self-imposed habits which have become practiced and accepted as truths. This requires help, guidance, and coaching from someone else more experienced.

Negativity as a Society

Humans not only embrace negativity individually, they do it collectively and as a society. In today's society, it is not uncommon to see faux groups banded together in the name of change, but the only real purpose is to perpetuate a cycle of negativity. This continues on into society. Negativity dominates news and even advertising. The reason a person needs to act now and buy something is to prevent a future condition which could be potentially life-threatening, or so they are led to believe.

Idealized Image and Conformity

This negativity has taken another subtler form as well, the idealized image of beauty in America. There has always been idealized imagery, from a housewife wearing pearls in the 60s, to the ideal image of a perfect size male and female as seen today in television, magazine, and online ads. It is a pressure exerted on society as a whole, a negative pressure, one that is related to conformity.

It is expected that a man and woman should look fit and be of a certain shape, get married at a certain age, be employed in specific types of careers, and have children - if they are considered to be happy, successful, and deserving of the best in life. This relates to the idealized or standardized image of who can hold hands in public, even though marriage laws in the United States have changed. Part of the reason for the persistent clinging to the old, idealized standard is the engrained negative belief structure held onto for so long by society and reinforced by religious institutions. This is a negative energy and is one which runs as a current through society and mankind.

Yet all of this continues, the negative energy streams, and somehow positive energy still exists. But to a person who is less than, which means someone who is less than perfect, less than the ideal standard, or less than in any way, how can they ever find acceptance in this world?

Finding Acceptance Among a Negative World

This is the primary problem: Trying to find acceptance in this world, or in this society, or in the external environment itself. No person can control any of these factors. There is only one form of self-acceptance. Once that can be found, it will not matter what society or religious institutions, or the world itself thinks, as a person will know true freedom.

So, what is self-acceptance and how does a person learn to embrace it? There is no amount of effort alone which can make this process occur and that is why the fad diets and gym plans do not work in the long term. Anything associated with additional negative energy, such as guilt, shame, must do, should do, or something similar, does not produce lasting change or self-acceptance. A person changes by learning to attune from within, and for many, this is a process which may take time.

Learning acceptance may likely take setbacks, frustrations, and challenges, as there must be events which wake a person up and cause them to examine their beliefs. When a person has gone on for so long, believing they are inadequate or unlikeable or unlovable, because of who they are or how they look, this creates deeply engrained thought processes which must be examined and changed. The way to do that is when something causes a time of reflection, often with challenges or frustration. When a person can begin to look within, after never having fully accepted who they are for whatever the reason may be, what usually happens is that they cannot find justification for feeling this way. Then they are mentally able to set themselves free.

If you have not yet reached this point in your journey, now is the time for you to think about why it is you feel the way you do. Yes, you can point to society or other external factors. But what is really holding you back from looking in a mirror now and fully embracing yourself, an energetic being in a physical form?

You created this life before you arrived. You designed this magnificent being. Could you really imagine a world where everyone looked all alike? What if every flower looked the same, how would you feel? The variety is what makes life interesting, exciting, fun, fresh, beautiful, and you are part of this now. You did not intend to be a clone. What is preventing you now from accepting who you are and how you look?

Learning to Live: Some Hopeful, Some Not

Self-acceptance requires making a conscious decision. It is not something a person tries to do and then decides to forget. By the time someone has reached a point where they are aware of how negative their belief systems have become, they will want to change.

But for some people, the change is not towards happiness and acceptance. Some people attune to the negative spectrum, which is when a person gives into depression, despair, or hopelessness. This person cannot accept who they are, or how they look, or care about who they are for any other set of reasons, and they cannot find anything positive to focus on. There is no sense of hope or they cannot find someone to help them, which means they cannot find a way to question the beliefs they are now holding.

Most people will have planned a life with challenges which prompt them to awaken from the negative beliefs they are holding at some point in their lives. When a person begins to accept who they are, how they look, or where they are at in life, true awakening can begin to occur. Acceptance is a positive energy and this is why it is associated with hope, love, renewal, and faith. It is also during this time of awakening that attunement brings greater clarity as the connection to the Collective Consciousness of mankind and Universal Wisdom becomes stronger, which means you are receiving new insight and guidance. You are feeling more positive, you are better focused, and you are more attuned to Universal Wisdom.

When you accept yourself, all of yourself, without the need for justification or the need for change, you open yourself to love, positive energy, and receiving wisdom from the inner voice which has been silenced for too long. Now you are beginning to live. Now you are alive.

Why Would Someone Choose to Live a Unique Life?

Do you feel as if you do not fit into the definition of "normal" as described by society, as if normal even exists? Have you ever been labeled "different" or "strange" or a "freak" by someone who deemed themselves better than you? Or do you find yourself not being accepted by religious institutions because of who you are or what you choose to believe?

It would seem as if society teaches us there is a standard definition of who is considered to be normal, and it is reinforced in magazines, movies, and television shows. Yet whenever someone is asked to define what normal means in society, the best description someone can describe usually refers to their skin color, physical condition, societal status or role, and overall appearance.

However, if you really examine society, it would be virtually impossible to create one definition of normal as there are literally endless variations of human exterior appearances. Yet the outdated idea of a normal man and woman does exist, especially with regards to looks.

What I was curious about was the idea of being normal from a perspective of other human characteristics, the qualities which make us unique. For example, as a gay man I grew up in a time period when it was not as socially acceptable and I had to struggle with my identity for many years. My response to what I was feeling was to hide my identity, until one day I decided to be true to myself and stop hiding. Even now, I still find I am cautious about revealing this truth to my employers. While marriage equality exists in the United States, workplace protections are not always guaranteed for all employees.

I then thought about many other people like me who must hide their identities for fear of retaliation on the job or are afraid of what other people might think of them. Once you state your truth, you cannot undo it. Then there are other types of unique people who struggle with human rights, beyond those who are gay, based upon their gender preference, skin color, or other qualities and characteristics. While the United States is one of the most advanced and progressive nations, many people struggle on a daily basis - either for their rights, to survive, or be treated as human beings.

This led me to the question I have as I focused on Universal Wisdom for guidance: Why would someone choose to live a unique life? I understand now that we choose our lives and create a plan before we arrive in a physical form. This means we must have an option to choose a physical form and a life which could be easy or difficult. I think about the number of losses, health challenges, career challenges, and the physical pain I have endured throughout my life, along with those I love, and I wonder why I would choose this type of path for my life - especially if I have decided to be a unique individual.

I realize this sounds as if being gay is a choice, which I will clarify. As someone in a physical form, you are who you are right now and you do not choose to be one way or another while in physical form. In other words, being gay is not a choice. But before you came into this physical form, I have come to understand that while you are in energetic form you can decide the life you want to live ahead of time, or before you come into this world, and this means you can choose to come into a physical form and be gay, or you can choose any other type of life you design.

I will share with you what I have learned about deciding to live a unique life, while connected to Universal Wisdom.

A universal truth is this: Every man, woman, and child begin their life with one unique physical characteristic, the fingerprint, which declares this person has their own identity in the world and cannot be claimed by someone else.

Other physical characteristics may be duplicated, such as hair style, skin tone, eye color, hair color, etc. The endless possible combinations create a world full of unique, special, interesting, vibrant, beautiful, and very human individuals.

There are also just as many interior characteristics possible as there are exterior characteristics. These interior qualities consist of emotions, a disposition, personality, intelligence, humor, wit, glow, charm, charisma, introvert, extrovert, and the hundreds of other names used to describe how a person behaves, feels, acts, responds, or thinks.

Establishing a Norm in Society

What society as a culture tends to focus on is the physical appearance. This has been done to create a norm, especially with regards to establishing standards of conduct for regulation and control of people. Religions decide who are normal and therefore worthy of receiving eternal life. Politicians decide who fit the societal norms and enact laws and regulations, or rights, privileges, and benefits for these groups accordingly.

This applies to all aspects of society, from food to fashion. There is an idealized standard of beauty, acceptable standards of a normal couple, standards of who can hold hands in public (typically male and female), a normalized look for clothes and fashion, and all of this is further reinforced in movies and television shows.

To think outside of these standards can make a person feel a sense of guilt or shame. To act outside of what is considered to be normal may result in ridicule, shaming, loss of a job, loss of family and friends, feelings of deep shame that are carried for a lifetime, and even worse than all of these conditions.

Living Outside of the Norm

When society treats people in this manner, groups, cliques, and memberships are formed. People tend to band together with others like themselves, which is why change eventually occurs for some groups over time - when a group grows large enough, is disenfranchised from the rest of society, and one day their voice is finally heard.

But more often than not, in a society that establishes strict definitions of normal, those who fall outside of the normal either try to fit in, or they join an outsiders group and stay in a fractured section of society. It is as if they are living in this world, but not accepted for who they really are - except by those who are outside of the norm with them. Those who fit in with societal expectations seem to have access to the best that can be acquired because they seemingly are rewarded.

The Myth of the Norm

In reality, the idea of a perfect norm in society is an illusion, along with anyone living a perfect life because they seemingly fit into that definition. Society constantly adapts over time because the people change and evolve, and they demand changes. Societal laws are always a battleground as politicians and other lawmakers can never win the ongoing battle of trying to control a diverse society by treating people as one type of person.

Even religions struggle to retain membership and followers because of using an outdated book, sources that were heavily edited to begin with as a means of controlling a particular civilization at the time it was put together. Yet this book is still used to this day, as a means of dictating morals, and exerting control over people.

The people who fall outside of the norm do not accept the attempt to be controlled so easily and that is why there is so much effort put into trying to control these groups - they do not easily comply with the ideas of trying to fit in, at least not in the long term.

Choosing or Not Choosing This Type of Life

By knowing all of these conditions, the question being sought is this: Why would someone want to be in this world, as a human being, and not fit in with society?

Here are some examples:

Why would someone choose to come into a physical form and be part of a minority group, only to experience prejudice?

Why would someone choose to come into a physical form and be gay, only to experience hate and discrimination, along with guilt and shame?

The answer begins first by remembering that you, and all human beings, begin as energy. When you choose a physical form you are still energy, and energy remains even after the physical form is shed. This means that what is most important is the energy, not the physical form.

The question needs to be changed to: Why does an energy source choose to add a physical form? That's the first question. The answer has to do with the sustaining and nurturing of the energy of life, or the source of life, the energy stream itself. The physical form creates memories, which is Collective Consciousness energy, the wisdom then nurtures Universal Wisdom. The emotions, both positive and negative, nurtures and sustains both ends of the spectrum of energy.

The second question then is this: How is a decision made about the type of physical form, along with the qualities and characteristics of the physical form? There are several factors. For example, if someone wants to come forward again and experience life in a different manner, this can influence their decision. Or if they are coming forward again with someone, those two energies will reach an agreement about the type of lives they want to experience. In other words, this is not a random process.

Choosing a Unique Life

Those who choose the most unique of lives to live are the ones who often get to experience the most in life itself. This is not to state it is the easiest life, as there may likely be hardships and challenges. Yet the unique nature of living outside of what is normally accepted as the standard for society can ultimately be the most rewarding. Some people will choose to come back later as well, after society has evolved, and their group or the nature of their unique qualities becomes more widely accepted. But often the challenges produce the most wisdom, which in turn nurtures Universal Wisdom, and ultimately, all of mankind.

A Unique Life vs. Individualism

What has been described is related to specific and identifiable characteristics or qualities, such as being gay or being part of a minority group. Other physical attributes which fall outside of the norm in society may never be fully embraced, and this is referred to as individualism.

When a person can express themselves, it means they trust their inner voice, they are tapped into their inner creativity, and they can sense the connection they have to Collective Consciousness - even if they do not understand what it means. A person who chooses to express their individuality may also find a life of challenges and struggle and live outside the established norm. While it can feel like a path no one should want to be on, it was a path chosen by design.

When you see someone, who appears to be outwardly unique, give them a smile. They may not yet be at a point in their journey where they recognize the path of fulfillment they have chosen; however, they may realize one day it is possible to achieve. A warm smile from you can help reassure them someone recognizes their journey.

If this person is you, part of your journey is self-acceptance. This alone may be a lifelong struggle as you learn to embrace the unique nature of your qualities. What makes you unique may be a combination of your personality and physical attributes. There is not one mold that anyone was made from because you determined all of the design specifics before you arrived in physical form. What matters most is that you remember the energy source you come from and you are still connected to at all times. This means you are following a plan and when you can find acceptance of yourself, you can begin to embrace your life's plan as well.

Who wants to be normal, when you can experience life to the fullest? Just by reading this now, it means you are well on your way to a journey of self-discovery, self-acceptance, and more importantly, self-transformation. *This is going to be an amazing life that you have planned for yourself.*

CHAPTER 2.
EVERYTHING IS ENERGY

What do you think of when you consider the universe and how it functions? Have you ever thought about what is powering the universe, the planets, or even just the Earth itself? There are elements we can experience as humans, such as feeling the winds blow and seeing the force of nature through a thunderstorm or observing the movement of the oceans. However, what is the power behind all of these living systems?

Those who were raised according to a strict religious indoctrination, and/or still subscribe to strict religious teachings, believe a God or supreme being is responsible for creating the universe and all living things. This viewpoint limits how a person sees the world and it isn't until these limiting beliefs are removed that someone is finally awakened and able to experience how life really functions. While some people decide or plan to hold onto their beliefs their entire life, others choose to break free and experience the joy of learning universal truths.

What you may not consciously think about or may never need to think about in your lifetime, is that everything in our world, along with everything in the universe, is a function and product of energy. There is one primary energy source that is the basis of all life. This energy source fuels the planets, and here on Earth it drives the winds, moves the oceans, and creates the weather. Even the functions of a human's body, including the automatic functions of the brain, all continue to exist and perform because of energy.

As a person begins to understand how energy fuels, nurtures, and supports every aspect of life, it then becomes possible to understand how humans exist as a result of this energy source. A person does not happen by accident or come into existence solely because of procreation. The origin of mankind in physical form is the energy source, which remains connected to each man, woman, and child until the physical form is shed. This connection to the energy source, referred to as a soul by religious institutions, also links each human to the Collective Consciousness of mankind, where all memories, knowledge, and wisdom is stored.

All of these topics will be addressed further in this chapter. What follows are the lessons I have learned about energy while accessing Universal Wisdom. The specific questions to be addressed in this chapter include: What is energy? What is the mind and body connection? What are names associated with energy? Is energy the same as God or a supreme being? What are the different forms of energy?

What is Energy?

Energy is one of the foundational laws of the universe. What I have learned in my journey is a universal truth and it is this: Energy is the source of all life, energy sustains life, life sustains energy, energy creates life, life generates energy, and the cycle continues without end. Some words used to describe energy include living, balanced, dynamic, nurtured, sustained, maintained, growing, powerful, energetic, and finite.

The energy source of life holds all of the memories of mankind. What you will read throughout this book, when energy is described, are energy spectrums. Positive memories are stored within the positive spectrum and negative memories are stored within the negative spectrum. Energy requires a balance of both positive and negative spectrums to sustain its balance.

The Dynamic Nature of Energy

Energy is infinite and the limits of the human mind are finite, even with a connection to the Collective Consciousness. This restricts fully understanding the nature and origins of energy and life, as a human cannot fully grasp how it came into being. What can be understood is that energy does not have a starting point or ending point. Energy exists through a tension of positive and negative signals, and those signals create a balance which sustains all of life.

Energy is constantly flowing, in and around all of mankind here on Earth, and it is also able to flow to and through connection points established with every living thing. It does not exist at an even, precisely measurable level, yet it is always available.

Energy is transmitted through signals that range in varying degrees from weak to strong, through the minds of all living things which act as the transmitters and receivers, establishing a direct connection to the source of life and Collective Consciousness of mankind. Energy can surge, fluctuate, and it can even be blocked at these connection points, depending upon mental barriers and internal filters.

Principles of Energy

Principle #1: Energy is without End

Every living thing requires some form of energy. Energy has always been. Energy is the source of life, a creator. As the intelligence of man grows, energy expands. This is the evolution of man and time. Energy is finite and has no end.

Principle #2: Energy is without Limits

Energy is in constant motion; it cannot be contained. Those who say they are able to harness it mean they have found a way to tap into it. For example, an electrician establishes a conduit and points of attraction so that it becomes a connection source.

Energy can also be sensed by those who are in healing professions. For example, a doctor can look for symptoms or conditions when a patient's body is not in normal alignment, or a therapist may be able to sense energy blockages during a massage.

Types of Energy

There are three types of energy: Static: That which does not move, Energetic: That which is in motion, and Magnetic: That which attracts like through vibration.

The human body can be static or in an energetic state. The human body's functions are energetic, always in motion, causing organs and molecules to move in a continuous flow.

The mind is magnetic and able to focus with clarity and attract similar thoughts, building momentum until what is focused upon become a manifestation. The mind can also exist in a state of flux, unfocused and moving from one scattered thought to the next. Every movement in the universe, down to every idea or thought, is all energy.

The Balance of Energy

A Universal Truth: Energy is balanced.

There isn't more positive energy than negative energy as it is all equal. In order for energy to be sustained, it must have an equal flow of positive and negative energy. As the positive energy spectrum and negative energy spectrum move towards the center, where they would meet, it is a neutral point that is neither positive or negative. It is from the neutral center that these two distinct "branches" are experienced, one flowing in a positive current and one flowing equally strong as a negative current.

There isn't a right or wrong with regards to types of energy, only degrees of energy. A person can choose either frequency. For example, a person can choose positive and experience ease and flow in their life. Or a person can also attune to negative energy and experience a wide variety of challenges and problems. Either choice can be correct as it all is a part of the balance of energy.

Those who seek to inspire others can do so by creating a shift in the vibration of the other person; however, they can only help to prompt a desire, they cannot actually change the vibration of someone else.

How does a person change their vibration and what they are attuned to? Through their primary transmitter, which is their brain. This can be accomplished with focus and directed thoughts.

What is the Mind and Body Connection?

Energy is automatic and cannot be turned off. It flows to and through the human body. A body that disconnects from it will experience what is called death. What is important to understand is this: Energy does not turn off and on, rather there is a connection or disconnection and it is the physical form or body that makes this connection or disconnection. An "on" switch makes the connection and an "off" switch disconnects.

When a decision is made to come forward from energy into a physical form, there is a connection made between the mind and body to the source of life energy. The mind and body will disconnect when the physical form sheds, yet the energy still exists as part of the Collective Consciousness of mankind.

A Sensory Experience

Energy in any form is felt or experienced in patterns and is a sensory experience for the human body. Those who are intuitive are those who have a highly developed awareness of energy. They can feel a shift in another person's energy pattern or flow. They are also receptive enough they can tune into the frequency of another person. Consider an electric outlet, which is connected to a source; it can energize anything that is receptive to it. This is similar to a person who is highly attuned to energy and able to sense the energy of others who are around them.

Energy can be sensed in a person's mood, experienced in their feelings, and expressed through their emotions. There are also degrees of tuning into the frequencies of energy. For example, a bad mood or an angry feeling indicates a person is attuned to the negative aspect of energy. In contrast, a good mood, happy feeling, or feeling of love is a matter of tuning to positive energy.

Someone who takes anti-depressants may not know how to feel or experience positive energy or hasn't practiced tuning to another frequency of energy other than the negative spectrum of energy.

To summarize: The body or physical form is a vessel, the mind is a conduit and creates a connection with the energy source of life, and the mind also transmits/receives signals to and from the Collective Consciousness of all of mankind.

The mind is the strongest of all conduits as it can receive and project energy. The mind uses thoughts to form a system of electrical circuits that are alive and pulsating at all times, even when sleeping.

Energy and Vibrations

A Universal Truth: Vibrations are receptors and transmitters of energy.

Consider this: Sound vibrates and is received through the senses of the human body. The mind is also vibrating, sending signals as transmissions. When energy vibrates from the mind, it does so in a subconscious manner. Some of this energy is directing functions of the human body and some of it retaining memories which become part of the Collective Consciousness within the energy life source.

In order to access the Collective Consciousness, a person needs to learn to attune their mind to the frequency of the positive spectrum and this source of knowledge. There are many teachers who have learned to do this; however, when they share knowledge they may attempt to control it and teach their followers to become dependent upon them. If a teacher will show you how to tune your mindset or share information with you without controlling you, you will experience the greatest benefit from listening to them.

When people speak of meditating or reflecting, they are allowing their minds to become a receptor. This means the mind is becoming attuned to the vibrating energy and seeking the signal of the Collective Consciousness. As a person thinks, creates, or develops new ideas, their mind is vibrating and transmitting signals of that knowledge or information, which is added to the Collective Conscious of mankind.

Vibrations from a person's mind are creating pathways to receive and transmit thoughts, ideas, and knowledge. The vibrations are providing signals, which are the direct carriers of thoughts or knowledge being conveyed or transmitted. What you may not consciously realize is that energy is constantly vibrating, without needing your direction or control, as all humans are part of the energy stream or energy source of life.

What a person can choose to do, with conscious effort, is to tune to the positive or negative components of energy. A person's mind is vibrating at all time, becoming receptive to ideas, impulses, or bursts of knowledge through signals received. When someone is thinking or developing ideas, they are transmitting knowledge through signals, as the mind is a transmitter.

The Flow and Balance of Energy

A Universal Truth: Energy flows from one living being to another.

Energy is sustained by the tension of positive and negative energy. It cannot be contained, it is always in motion, it cannot be controlled, it is transmitted to and from humans through vibrations, it is received through conduits such as the mind, and energy can flow from one being to another. However, in order for energy to flow from one person to another, it must be focused in some form which can be received with one of the five senses by the receiver.

Here is an example: The sender can use a touch, gesture, sound, or even a thought as a mode of transmitting energy. The receiver must be attuned to the sender to accept and understand the energy being transmitted. In contrast, the touch of a stranger would likely go unnoticed and unacknowledged, and the energy would not flow, if the person is not attuned to the other person in some manner.

When two people form a close relationship, they have actually become practiced being attuned to each other, which allows their energy to flow easily to and from each other. What is referred to as love is a connection of energy which is being experienced as a strong current. The connection through the mind as a conduit is the strongest, as the mind has a direct connection to the bodily functions, and this allows a person to demonstrate not only an emotional but also a physical response to another person.

To maintain a loving relationship, there needs to be sustained energetic connection between the people within the relationship. This requires an active focus and the flowing of energy from one being to another. And just like all energy, there is a positive and negative aspect. A person can be closely attuned to negative energy and in doing so, project it to the person they are in close relationship with because of the connection established with this other person or persons.

When one person states the other is no longer the same person, it means their flow and transmission of energy has changed. Those who are in a relationship may still have a connection, but it is weakened if they are not both focused on the same energy source.

What Are Names Associated with Energy?

Most people do not think about energy itself or how it is the source of life. People are accustomed to believing in a higher power from the perspective of a supreme being or the universe as a source itself.

Few believe, or are willing to believe, the energy of life is the force or source which nurtures and supports all of mankind. There have been a variety of names given to explain the source of life energy, from infinite intelligence to God.

Infinite Intelligence

Energy connects and retains the intellect of mankind and therefore has been called Infinite Intelligence. Energy can retain images, words, and anything else referred to as memory. Intelligence is a form of focused energy that has been harnessed or channeled for a specific purpose. Since intelligence is stored in the Collective Consciousness, it is infinite in nature. While the phrase Infinite Intelligence is used by some teachers, in place of a supreme being, it can be traced back to Napoleon Hill almost 100 years ago.

A Life Force

Energy is all around us, and so it has been called a Life Force. Those who could not define it saw it as a higher being, an advanced power, a force greater than humans, and called it a Supreme Being, gods of many names, the one God, or other spiritual entities.

It seemed if something was in existence before and after the birth and death of a human, therefore it must be an entity who is controlling the universe. It must also mean, or at least it was later inferred by some, that this entity also controlled the destiny of man.

Good and Evil

Energy, or the manifestations of the energy spectrums, has been called "good" because of its pure nature and "evil" because of the negative fluctuations and variance in levels.

Energy, with its positive and negative currents, is used as an analogy for good and evil: It is referred as "good" because the positive energy spectrum has absorbed the intellect and best of mankind. It is also referred to as "bad" as the negative spectrum attracts anything considered to be destructive and harmful to humans.

This is the reason why there are categories defined as good or bad, they are opposite forms of energy. When anything is experienced from only the negative spectrum, this is when the "bad" or painful or less than desirable emotions or feelings are experienced. In contrast, positive energy, or anything experienced from only the positive spectrum, creates pleasant emotions. Both of these spectrums are needed to create a dynamic form that sustains the energy of life. Both exist and together create a balance.

It is not possible for a person to live without negative energy, which means there are going to be sensory moments, or feelings that vary from pleasant to unpleasant. Someone who is emotional is prone to experience both spectrums. A fluctuation towards negative energy can and will be felt. A person with emotional control has learned to tune their frequency towards positive energy or change their point of focus.

Source Energy

There are teachers who refer to energy as Source Energy. Adding the word "Source" seems to give it a sense of authority. Simply stating that "you are connected to energy" does not sound as dramatic as telling someone they are connected to Source Energy.

But it is energy, an energy stream we are all connected to. It is a source, the source of all life. It is a consciousness of all living and non-living, with a higher order Universal Wisdom, which is available to call upon, and has been called Infinite Intelligence.

Teachers of Law of Attraction often talk about the way in which "Source Energy" operates - how it experiences life through humans, how humans are an extension of Source, how Source creates manifestations by arranging cooperative components, and how Source knows what you want and waits for the right timing. One teacher has stated that "Source has your back".

If you look closely at all of those teachings, you see there is a common thread of someone or something else still being in control of your life or your destiny. This is no different than the way religion teaches energy - it is about a higher power dictating terms or controlling human destiny. What if Law of Attraction teachers do this to create dependency on them? Or what if they do not trust their followers to be able to handle or want the actual truth?

Energy is the Source

I wanted to better understand the concept of Source Energy, as I have heard this phrase used by teachers of Law of Attraction. This created a powerful question within me, which caused me to focus even more deeply while I have been connected to Collective Consciousness and higher order Universal Wisdom.

What I have begun to learn is a complex topic and one I am only beginning to understand. At times I find it challenging to write my notes as Universal Wisdom exceeds my human understanding and vocabulary, and the wisdom I am tapping into is so immense I know I am only touching a tip of what humans have access to as a whole. This is what I have begun to learn about energy and the meaning of Source Energy.

The phrase "Source Energy" is helpful for some people as a means of understanding the Laws of the Universe. To say "Source Energy" can be confusing for others as it would seem to imply a person must find it. But energy is all around us. It is the source of life. Energy can be experienced through focus and the transmission of thoughts. The mind and the brain are transmitters of energy, receivers of energy, and use energy to sustain life.

A Universal Truth: Energy Exists.

No one controls the energy of life, making decisions as to how it flows, or how much or how often. Energy doesn't have a source. People refer to energy in terms of source energy, as if you could tap into more or receive more. There are frequencies and degrees of energy. Energy can be felt strong through powerful emotions or powerful forces in nature. Energy can also be steady or a constant force. For example, when a person is sitting by a lake and experiences a feeling that is described as peaceful and calm.

A person can tune into varying degrees of energy and this is where "source energy" comes into common phrasing. What it actually means is having an awareness of the energy that surrounds you. When you consider how life around you can be sustained, you are focusing on the "source" of life, which is energy. There is only one source, the energy that sustains life.

A Supreme Being

As the very idea of a Supreme Being, a God, someone who was in control of the universe, grew with time - the next natural evolution of thought was to describe this Supreme Being. Look at various cultures and how different or similar those descriptions may be. For example, Greeks had gods, while Native Americans had spirits and totems. Organized religion created a persona, an image, and created stories - even creating a book of stories that followers would hold onto for hundreds of years, believing these stories to be true, no matter how outdated it might become.

Religious institutions even created a persona to represent the opposite of positive energy, which is negative energy, and a devil or evil entity was born. The evil image was complete with horns and a pitchfork to symbolize negative energy. Then there were bad behaviors associated with this evil image, along with consequences for not obeying the right set of laws and rules.

Is Energy the Same as God or a Supreme Being?

The energy which nurtures and sustains life is capable of doing so without the direct involvement of humans, and this is the reason why people believe there is a higher power. This is also why energy has been called a supreme being, with people who make statements that they are an authority as to how access to the supreme being, who is worthy to access the divine, and who can best interpret the knowledge received.

As man has come to understand energy, a name had to be given to it to explain what it is and this is how words such as "God" and "source" came to be. The word "God" was associated with positive energy as this spectrum produces feelings of love and joy and vitality and peace. When someone is focused or attuned to positive energy, and something in their life changes, it can appear that miracles have happened.

But then there is negative energy and a vibration focused on what seems to be the worst of mankind. A character named the "devil" was developed, an extension of the word "evil", as a means of creating fear for that type of energy. Later that word "devil" was used to create control over others, along with conditions to overcome it, as if it can be avoided to begin with.

Negative energy will always exist. It is not inherently evil but a function or process which creates a balance, one that is needed for life energy to be sustained. When people experience what they believe are bad or evil circumstances, they pray. What they are doing is creating a vibrational shift, or an attempt to change their circumstances. When they are able to shift their vibration, and a change occurs, they may believe "God" has heard them and answered their prayers. In reality, what they did they were able to do on their own and that was create a shift in their vibration to a positive energy spectrum.

What Does It Mean to Have a Soul?

A Universal Truth: Every human is energy, created from energy, created by energy, sustained by energy, connected to energy, and nurtured by energy in return.

Mankind has made a mystery out of an existence which is man. Instead of accepting the fact all humans are energy and the source of energy, the idea of a soul was created - as if there are two parts of a human, which there are not. A human being appears solid yet is a walking and living and breathing energetic form. The feeling of having a soul or separate existence inside is the consciousness, the source of connectedness to higher order Collective Consciousness and Universal Wisdom. But the two are not separate.

When someone "dies" it means a shift has occurred on a cellular level. The cells have shed and all that remains is the pure unseen energy. This is why it may seem as if houses or places are haunted, as there are energy traces left behind. Metals can retain energy, along with certain minerals. The metals and materials within homes can retain some of the memories and energies of occupants who lived have lived there.

There has been much built around the idea of a soul - so much so that it has become engrained in our culture. You will hear or read people talk about taking care of the soul, nurturing the soul, or refer to the heart and soul of someone or something. It is meant to refer to the essence of the being of someone.

But a soul seems to add to the idea of separation between man and the source of life, when there is none. This is common with religion. Man is separated from a supreme being and must atone, living according to a prescribed philosophy in order to achieve the ultimate prize - residency in an imaginary golden palace in the sky, floating around, worshipping the supreme being who deemed them worthy to be there.

When you closely examine the very idea of what is being told to the masses, it is so incredulous that it seems hard to imagine it has been sustained for so long. Yet it has, as people want someone else to be in charge. Few ultimately want the responsibility for knowing they are the source, that they are the ones in control, and only they can make changes. It is more comfortable to believe someone else is in charge, follow a set of prescribed rules based upon the selected religious affiliation, and then hope eternal access to happiness is granted. All you know is that you do not want your immortal soul burning in a pit of flames for eternity because you slipped up once or twice along the way. You will keep trying as best you can.

If you think about trying to live like that, it can be exhausting. That is why there are so many part-time believers, and those who turn to religion only in times of need. The best time to gain compliance from humans is during the greatest need, when prayers consist of begging. But all of this is bondage. It is a system, just like any other institution, a means of societal control. It is not reality. If it were, there would not be so many different versions of what is believed to be the truth.

There is but one truth: Man is energy, a powerful being, a source of life, knowledge, and wisdom, with access to greater wisdom and knowledge. To know there is no separation between you and the source of life energy, to know you are part of the source, to know what you have access to, and to know you are energy in physical form, changes everything for a human.

You can awaken to the world around you. This is when you finally come alive. There is no praying to someone else. There is only you, in control of your life and your access, with access to greater, divine and inspired knowledge. Your purpose is not to live according to someone else's rules for some afterlife prize, or fail and be condemned, your purpose is to live. That is why you came. That is why you are here.

Who Am I Praying To?

Has life ever felt too unbearable for you? Have you reached a point where you believe nothing was going your way and you experienced utter hopelessness? Do you look at the circumstances of your life now and wonder how it will ever get better, or if you will ever finally get a break? Or do you feel as if your life has now passed you by and all you have experienced are challenges and pain, and you want nothing more than to change every aspect of it - but do not know how to make it happen on your own?

There are many times in a person's life when circumstances and events can cause deep feelings of sadness, hopelessness, and even despair. When this happens, there may be an inclination to turn within and withdraw or reach out for help. I was raised in an environment as a young person where I was taught to pray and ask for divine assistance any time I needed help or guidance. I hoped this supreme being would be willing to listen to me and provide assistance, but I also knew I had to live according to certain conditions or else my prayers might go unanswered - or worse, I would be punished.

This idea of praying was so deeply engrained in me as a young person that being gay created deep conflict within me, so much so I spent my early adulthood hiding the truth and living a lie. I lived in fear of being punished and had fear of not having my prayers answered. Yet deep within me, I could feel something was not right about what I had been taught as I knew if I meditated, I could focus on something which allowed me to discover different truths. The problem was the information I gained during meditation was vastly different than the religious teachings I was given, especially as related to the idea of who the supreme being is, and it deepened my internal conflict.

The first set of mental barriers and limiting beliefs I had to remove were those involving my authentic self. I had to live my truth, which meant getting a divorce and coming out. This did not happen until I was in my 30s. It took me that long to finally overcome all of the rhetoric and demeaning language I had learned as an impressionable young person. This was not an easy time period in my life and it took a while to complete, but I did it and once I came out, I never looked back - and I never wanted to either.

The next step in my transformation was trying to understand what I was experiencing while I was meditating. I knew I was gaining insight and knowledge, but I did not understand what it was I was tapping into. I also never thought of it as meditating as I was not one to sit on a yoga mat and practice quiet reflection, but I do listen to ambient music and write in journals, which is my way of tapping into the limitless part of my mind. It was in my 40s when I discovered the Law of Attraction, and Law of Attraction teachers, and this propelled my next significant transformation - until I finally outgrew their teachings and readied myself to become a teacher of Laws of the Universe.

Now I understand what I have always been able to do naturally, which anyone can train themselves to do, and it is to tap into the Collective Consciousness of mankind and access Universal

Wisdom. As a teacher of Laws of the Universe I now seek out knowledge to help answer questions I have about life, and I share this to help others who may also have the same questions.

Yet I still find myself faced with challenges in life, just as anyone might, and I wonder during those moments when someone believes they need divine assistance or help from a supreme being: Who is this people are praying to, especially if they believe their prayers are being answered?

I ask these important questions as I have come to understand the Laws of the Universe, and through this knowledge I know there isn't a being who is dictating control of the source of life. Yet the idea of prayer and faith is so deeply engrained in mankind, I wanted to better understand its purpose.

I will share what I have learned about prayers, and prayers being answered, while I was connected to Universal Wisdom.

A universal truth is this: Mankind has been taught, through years of deep conditioning, not to trust the natural or instinctual voice that resides within, the voice which is the transmission or connection to the Collective Consciousness of all of mankind. Humans, for the most part, do not believe they can possess the wisdom or knowledge they need to address questions, problems, and challenges in their lives. More importantly, humans are kept from believing they can have direct access to the source of knowledge and wisdom needed to live their lives in a fulfilled and satisfying manner.

Being Taught to Be a Dependent Follower

Humans have been taught there must be an intermediary, or someone who can access this knowledge on their behalf. Those intermediaries consist of priests, pastors, shamans, spiritualists, popes, teachers, or anyone who puts themselves in a position of stating they have special access to a divine knowing, a special or unique understanding to life and the source of knowledge of life, or anyone else who claims to know the mysteries and answers to life.

For example, this could be a priest who states they are allowed to communicate with God for their followers, or a Law of Attraction teacher who claims to channel a higher source of knowledge or wisdom for their followers. Either way is presenting information via a perceived unique pathway as a chosen vessel, continuing the fallacy that humans must be loyal subjects and await their next outpouring of words.

But that is not how it should be. Anyone who can access Universal Wisdom and share it as a teacher, or with any other title, can have the most transformative impact by showing how everyone has access to this knowledge, not just a chosen or privileged few. But the conditioning and teaching practices are tightly held.

Developing Learned Helplessness

When humans do not trust they have the natural insight, knowledge, or wisdom, or they question what they instinctually know inside because they have been taught dependency for so long, humans may develop a sense of learned helplessness when faced with challenging situations and circumstances that cannot be easily resolved on their own. Some people may choose to ask family or friends for help or advice at that time, and this may or may not be helpful, depending upon the intent of the assistance provided.

Quite often the more people who become involved in helping a person who feels challenged and helpless, the more difficult it can become to see clearly while trying to find an answer or resolve an issue. This may ultimately lead to increased frustration.

Feeling Hopelessness and Needing to Pray

When a person is faced with a situation that is too great, feels too overwhelming, or is more than anyone else can possibly assist them with, this is when a sense of despair, depression, or even hopelessness may begin to set in. It is during this time when a person may feel inclined to pray in earnest, to even plead if the circumstances are dire or an answer is needed quickly. If a person believes they have not lived their life "right" or in accordance with what their religious institution prescribes, they may need to first repent and promise to never veer off course again. This is part of the conditioning for many faith-based religions, knowing there is a vengeful God.

Next, there may be some bartering or negotiating involved in the prayers, a promise made to do something if the prayer is answered quickly. This entire premise operates under the assumption that prayers work in this manner and that someone or something is in control of the universe, evaluating the requests of billions of people, to try to determine who is worthy, whose prayers should go unanswered or ignored, and who should be punished for not following the rules.

None of this is based in reality. It is part of religious conditioning, which has been handed down from one generation to the next, accepted without any questions. Yet when a person is in need, facing a challenge in their life, and they pray - what is that really doing for them? They are doing nothing other than waiting and hoping for a sign, or a miracle, or a resolution. This never teaches them they hold the knowledge within.

When a person waits for a prayer to be answered, and they receive nothing, what happens then? This person may become even more frustrated, upset, and feeling hopeless. And all of this time, they could have accessed the Collective Consciousness and Universal Wisdom if they had known how to and relieved their suffering much more quickly.

What Does Praying Really Mean?

What humans do not realize is this: When they pray, it is really their natural instinct trying to reach out to the Collective Consciousness of mankind, to access the knowledge and wisdom needed. But most humans are not taught they can actually do this and most do not know about it or believe it is even a possibility.

But it is a natural instinct. This is how the mind was programmed as it is still connected to the energy source of life. Humans were energy before coming forward in a physical form. While in a physical form, the energy source is still connected. But it is possible to create mental barriers to prevent natural or instinctual processes from occurring.

Here is an example: A person is facing a life crisis. There are many possible reactions taken. Here are two of the possible options which may be considered at this point.

Option #1. The person may feel a need to pray and seek divine assistance or help from a supreme being. They understand they may have to repent, try to barter as part of the process, and then they must wait for an answer or sign of the prayer being answered - if it will be answered at all.

Option #2. The person may believe in Law of Attraction and follow a teacher of Law of Attraction. This person knows that according to Law of Attraction, they must think thoughts of happiness and well-being to attract like thoughts. But they do not feel either at this point and under these circumstances. This teacher may also have this person believe they have to await source energy to align cooperative components to attract the right answers and open the pathway.

Both options create dependency on someone or something else, and ultimately teach helplessness, when the answers are within each and every person.

It's Not Really About Who You Are Praying To

The act of praying itself can help to calm some people down and put them in a meditative state. If that happens, the natural innate connection to the source of life energy can flow, and access to wisdom is gained. There may be flashes of insight received during this state, which will make it feel as if the prayers were answered.

For both examples given above, praying to a supreme being or waiting on source energy, a person is waiting on someone or something to resolve their challenges. Answers may come about, but not as a result of praying to a supreme being or through source energy aligning cooperative components.

You may also receive answers and wisdom for challenges in your life through insight, such as an "aha" moment, when you feel "I have an idea", or something similar. It happens when a person turns inward and becomes quiet, often referred to as being sad or depressed. This is actually a quieting time, when a person only knows how to express what they are feeling through the use of prayers.

But it is not about who a person is praying to as this is a conditioned practice. It is a matter of learning to believe that anyone can have access to the wisdom and knowledge needed, any time it is needed, and the source of this information is available without restriction. The wisdom of all of mankind resides in the Collective Consciousness, stored in the source of life energy, which all humans have unrestricted access to at any time.

This is not to state that religions or Law of Attraction teachers do not have their place. Anyone who has wisdom to share can be of value to others, provided they share information rather than try to control it. No human needs to live in fear of being able to access the wisdom of man or need anyone to access it for them. There is no one supreme being controlling humans as religions teach. There is a source of life, one which is an energy source, and all humans are connected to it at all times. It is through this source that wisdom is accessed, received, and available to guide all humans.

When you feel challenged, do not be concerned with the method you use to find internal reflection. If you feel the need to pray, pray. But use your prayers not as pleading to a divine being but as a sense of tuning your internal vibration to the source of life energy, to seek the wisdom of mankind. It is then you will find answers and relief, without fear of being judged, controlled, or rejected for seeking this wisdom. You are part of the source of life, the energy of all of mankind. You are always worthy to receive the wisdom and knowledge of all of mankind, just as you are free to be and believe.

What Are the Different Forms of Energy?

Energy is the source of all forms of life and it fluctuates, grows, expands, and sustains. Here are examples of energy: the body and mind, nature, money, economics, time, and thoughts. Energy is the source of ideas, inspiration, intuition, emotions, feelings, words, language, sight, sound, taste, touch, writing, singing, and laughing. One of the most important forms of energy for human beings, is love.

Learn About the Endless Energy of Love

Love is a positive energy, allowing humans to develop deep connections with each other. This form of energy can be sustained as a connection throughout time, even when the physical form is gone.

A Universal Truth: The energy of love cannot be contained.

Love is an energetic connection. The transmitting signal may be weak, strong, or anywhere in between. People stay in that pattern of love as long as they maintain a vibrational match or signal. The longer people become practiced being attuned to each other, through focus of vibration, the stronger the connection grows. The connection between people that flows energy to and from each other is experienced through the senses, and a positive connection is expressed through feelings of happiness and bliss.

It is possible for an energetic connection between two people to be so strong it transcends the physical form. Once the physical form is gone, memories become a permanent part of the Collective Consciousness. A strong bond or connection between people can create new life experiences once again, and the memories come back into new human forms, allowing the connection to continue through a new life together with new memories. It is even possible to come back again together, over and over.

For two or more people to come back together again, there must be an agreement made while part of the Collective Consciousness. The vibrational connection that will be sustained comes forward in new human form. A decision will have been made as to how much to remember from past life memories and how much life to experience individually before reconnecting.

Lessons Learned

When someone is born, they are a product of energy flowing into a new form. There are many forms which exist, and not one form can ever contain the whole of the life energy. Every living thing, including all human beings, come as an extension of the energy source. Energy creates life and connects all of life. Energy retains thoughts and memories; no one begins as a blank slate when they are born. Everyone is connected to the energy source. Some people are more aware of the Collective Consciousness they have access to, and this includes writers, artists, actors, and many others who are in creative fields.

Everyone has access to the benefit and wisdom of mankind, a collective energy stream of thoughts. It is a matter of learning to focus and tuning the mind to receive vibrational impulses. A person who is destitute is tuned to the negative end of the spectrum of energy, where thoughts of failure and despair reside. This is the vibrational pattern of those who are depressed and feeling hopeless.

For those who can tune to the positive spectrum of energy, they receive insight and inspiration. They can seemingly come up with endless ideas, and the longer they maintain such a practiced fine tuning, the easier it becomes for them, and they receive the flow of positivity easily. For those who look to others to tell them how to behave or act, their vibrational signal or connection to the energy source is not as strong as someone who has practiced listening to their voice. Within the inner quiet mind is the vibrational conduit for collective wisdom.

The following principles will read throughout this book:

Everything is energy: All humans are connected to the source of life of energy.

Humans decide how to shape their experience: This occurs by design prior to arrival, and with insight provided through dreams and visions, and steps or elements of the plan revealed in the right time.

While here, there is access to the Collective Consciousness: When needed, anyone can accomplish this through focus or being attuned, as it is possible to tap into higher order Universal Wisdom.

When something is desired: Law of Attraction can be used in conjunction with other Laws of the Universe, such as Law of Connection or Law of Presence. But there is not one law which provides all the answers to life. Every person is in direct control of his or her own life, and has a plan created for their life. Whenever wisdom is sought, this is the time to see wisdom and insight from within, to listen for guidance from the Collective Consciousness of mankind and higher order Universal Wisdom.

To live an empowered and enlightened life: You need to know there is a source of life energy, universal truths, universal laws, a Collective Consciousness, and higher order Universal Wisdom.

Humans do not need to look for a supreme being: A supreme being is not guiding or shaping how humans live. Humans dictate and create their own life experiences. The Laws of the Universe are guidelines or parameters for how the Collective Consciousness is accessed and maintains the energy stream and connection to human existence. When humans are enlightened and connected to the Collective Consciousness of mankind, they can receive wisdom and knowledge to guide their lives. They can also receive insight into the plan they have created, to live fulfilling and happy lives.

There is no Source of life to seek out because humans are connected to and part of the source of life energy.

CHAPTER 3.
COLLECTIVE CONSCIOUSNESS

It is easy for you to accept and believe there are planets in the universe because you can see them. You may also accept there is a supreme being or higher power who created this universe because you were told so, as a matter of faith, even without ever having seen this supreme being or higher power. But is it possible that what you were told by religious leaders, and what you have accepted as a matter of fact, is not how the universe was created or how it operates?

If you have continued to read what has been written here, then there is something within you that is curious to know more and it is part of an awakening process. This is a time when you begin to look at the customs, beliefs, and teachings you accepted throughout your life and ask: Are these beliefs valid? Should I continue to accept these beliefs? Are these beliefs and teachings reality, or do I innately know there is more to life than what I have been taught by my family, schools, and religious institutions?

I also went through this process and for me, I could always feel the conflict from within, even during the time in my life when I hid my authentic self. Deciding to question your beliefs and belief systems can certainly feel uncomfortable at times, but once you make a decision to find answers, and you finally liberate your inner being - there is such joy and peace to be felt you will never imagine a time before it.

To help you get started, here are some initial questions to ask yourself, which you may or may not need to answer at this point in your journey:

When you are thinking right at this very moment, are those thoughts all yours?

When you hear or read something, how do you store, retain, and later recall all of that information? Is all of it coming strictly from inside of your mind?

When you have what is referred to as an "aha" moment, is that your idea, originating from inside of your mind?

If you believe in a supreme being and you pray, and you receive an answer or guidance, where did it come from and how did you receive it?

If you believe you have a soul, how does it stay within your body? How does that soul know to stay there and wait until the very moment of your death? Is it possible this soul of yours is connected to other souls?

It is helpful to consider these questions, if you want to begin to see other possibilities beyond what you have been told or accepted as truths throughout your life.

The Energy Source of Life

What you have read about in this book is that energy is the source of all life. This energy of life is a magnetic field, an invisible current which is running through and around all of us, all of life, and all of the universe.

Physical forms here on Earth come from this magnetic field yet are still connected to this energy source by the mind. The mind transmits, receives, and vibrates signals. The next logical question is this: If humans are still connected to the energy of life, the source of life itself, what is it that humans are connected to?

Collective Consciousness

Humans are connected to a Collective Consciousness. This is a living organism comprised of energy; living matter which is evolving and growing. It is a repository of thought signals and receives all of the memories from all of mankind. It is similar to a library with all of mankind's thoughts embedded into energetic form, accessible by any human through the mind.

The Energy Spectrums

Within Collective Consciousness a duality exists, as there are two spectrums: a positive energy spectrum and a negative energy spectrum. Both of these spectrums are needed to sustain and balance the source of life energy.

The Positive Energy Spectrum: Words that can be used to describe the positive energy spectrum include happy, successful, enlightened, awakened, winning, evolving, believing, hopeful, inspired, motivated, and alive.

The Negative Energy Spectrum: Words used to describe the negative energy spectrum include doubt, fear, nervous, scared, upset, worried, hopeless, afraid, sad, failure, pain, depression, loss, and decline.

Higher order, Universal Wisdom

From the positive energy spectrum, higher order, universal wisdom evolves. This is the wisdom of all of mankind, and includes some of the following examples: Lessons Learned, Trial and Error, Life's Experiences, Hindsight, Wisdom of the Ages, Benefit of Age, Knowledge, Advanced Education, Advanced Experience, Advanced Training, Teachings from Teachers and Educators

To access Universal Wisdom, it requires a person to have a practiced vibration of being attuned or focused on the positive energy spectrum, as it is from the positive energy spectrum that Universal Wisdom flows.

Our Connection to Collective Consciousness

What I know is that man gave the Collective Consciousness names such as God, Source, Infinite Intelligence, among others. Yet that takes away from the nature of the energy we are all part of and have access to. If we are experiencing emotions from the negative spectrum, we need to attune to the positive spectrum by changing our vibrational signal or focus to positive emotions. From a positive focus we can all gain insight and wisdom. We may not be able to affect immediate change in our situations or circumstances, as a result of the plan we have established, but we can gain peace, understanding, and relief from the negative emotions.

It is also possible that gaining knowledge from Universal Wisdom, at any point in a person's life, will be so transformative that changes do occur. This means that elements of your life's plan can begin to open up or you are now clear-minded and you can see what steps to take to make your plan a reality. One thing that being attuned to the positive energy spectrum, and listening for insight from Universal Wisdom certainly does, is to put you back in control. You are now in control of your thoughts and emotions, rather than living in a spinning cycle of negativity. You are also not relying on someone to be an intermediary and access this knowledge for you.

My ability as a teacher of Laws of the Universe is to focus and listen, without doubt or questions, to seek knowledge and believe in what I am receiving. I can now quickly attune to Universal Wisdom. I will share with you what I have learned about the Collective Consciousness while attuned to Universal Wisdom.

A universal truth is this: The brain is the complex center of a living system, creating the systemic neural network through which the mind is allowed to operate, performing the automatic functions of the body. Without the brain, there is no mind, and the physical form or body ceases to exist.

Now consider this perspective: The physical form or body without a brain cannot come to life. There is no way for the body to generate impulses to direct its functions, and more importantly, there is no way for the body to produce energy.

The body needs energy to sustain itself, no matter what condition the body may be in, whether perfect of imperfect. The entire body is an energetic state and it is a product of the mind generating a system of thoughts and commands through the brain's network.

The universe itself operates in a similar manner. It is all a matter of energy. Energy creates and energy sustains. Energy sustains life and energy is the source of life itself. There have been names given to this energy source, and misconceptions developed about it. This was done for a variety of reasons, but primarily due to the religions needing to dictate terms and exert control. It was also believed man could not easily accept the universal truth about the order of the universe, and this is how a system of religious restrictions was put into place.

People want to believe someone is responsible for how life began and how their lives came into existence, which means this is the entity they can turn to in times of need. To suggest man is operating by a life they created, and any help they need they must access on their own, could be too much for a human's mind.

How the Universe Operates

But the reality is this: The universe functions like the human or animal or any other life form. It needs energy to survive, and the energy comes about as a result of impulses directed by the mind, through the brain.

For the universe, there is no physical form, but there are physical forms, consisting of planets such as Earth. The "brain" so to speak, for the universe, is the Collective Consciousness of all of mankind. It isn't a physical brain, but an energetic brain, one which generates energy and physical forms. The Collective Consciousness stores, retains, transmits, and receives signals and vibrations from the minds of all living things.

Energy is all around the universe, ever present, invisible to the human eye, but permeating every aspect of every living thing. Collective Consciousness, the repository of all thoughts and memories of mankind, resides within this universal energy. It is the sources of life for the energy of the universe, nurturing it as new physical forms are generated, and being nurtured as humans generate new thoughts. It is a self-perpetuating cycle. There is no way the energy of the universe could end, unless every single living thing in the universe was eliminated, and the energy itself was extinguished, which could never happen.

Thoughts Forms and Collective Consciousness

The Collective Consciousness repository has a negative and positive spectrum, as is the nature of energy. As the thoughts of humans are thought through the minds of humans, those thought forms are automatically drawn to the associated spectrum. There is no one in charge of these spectrums, and there is no one who is sorting these thoughts. No one is in charge of the repository either. That is why the writer of this book has access now, anyone can tap into it, if they are attuned.

But thoughts of humans carry a vibration with it, positive or negative, whether or not it is recognized. For example, as a person thinks, they either think from a positive, negative, or neutral position. The negative thoughts, associated with emotions such as pain, grief, sadness, etc., are immediately drawn to the negative spectrum. The converse is true of thoughts such as happiness, joy, excitement, pleasure, etc., which are drawn to the positive spectrum.

Collective Consciousness and Universal Wisdom

As human beings experience life there is more going on than just thinking thoughts. Humans are also learning, adapting, growing, gaining wisdom, and so on. This advanced knowledge or information is more than just thoughts being generated by a person's mind. This is insight, and more importantly, wisdom which is being gained.

The Collective Consciousness of mankind has this wisdom stored in a repository separate from the energy spectrums. It is a product of, and accessed through, the positive energy spectrum. It was designed this way to provide humans with a place to turn for answers when they wanted to help themselves. Only a small percentage of the human population would be willing to attune and search on their own, yet the wisdom is there for all to access or receive.

The reason Universal Wisdom is accessed through the positive spectrum is that negative feelings and emotions would create mental barriers to being able to attune to this wisdom. A positive vibration is the highest vibrational signal possible for a human. Universal Wisdom allows the best of mankind to be stored and retained, never lost, available for all of mankind to access now and in the future. What is drawn to the positive and negative spectrums are energetic thought forms and serve to fuel the energy of life. But those energy spectrums are not meant to be accessed and explored by humans.

When humans describe having an active memory, and are remembering past memories in great detail, that is coming from their own mind, not the Collective Consciousness. When a human has active past memories, it means the person has lost focus or is feeling strong emotions related to the negative spectrum, which draws in and traps a person in a cycle of what is often described as pain and regret.

The negative and positive spectrums of Collective Consciousness are not meant to be tapped into. When a person meditates or is concentrating, they are seeking knowledge and wisdom, and they are attempting to attune to Collective Consciousness and Universal Wisdom. Many will not know what it is they are tapping into, rather they will feel what seems like insight, ideas, fresh creativity, and inspiration. Some may believe a divine or supreme being is conversing with them.

No matter what a person believes, or what they believe they are entitled to, every person has access to Universal Wisdom. All of mankind is connected to the Collective Consciousness. No one is ever cut off. No one is judged worthy or not. There is no one controlling it from the perspective of a supreme being.

Collective Consciousness and The Essence of a Person's Life

The brain of the energy of the universe is the Collective Consciousness. All of the thought forms create an energy source which keeps it flowing and from it, physical life evolves. The mind of the Collective Consciousness consists of the thoughts, signals, and vibrations which are transmitted and received from life forms.

The energy source of life also stores the essence of a person's life. This is how a person retains a consciousness once the physical form is gone, and then how they can return again in another physical form. These life essences of mankind are formed as part of the Collective Consciousness. But at the nucleus of Collective Consciousness are the positive and negative energy spectrums, serving as the generator for the universal source of life. The life essence forms, the metaphysical forms which no longer have a physical form here on Earth, create a network which are available for communication with each other.

What these conscious essence forms contain are the essential characteristics, personalities, and memories relevant to the establishment of who this person was or has been in physical form or forms on Earth. This allows them to decide if they want to return again with those same memories, if they want to return with someone again or someone else or start from a new perspective. If a person chooses a new perspective, they can decide upon the circumstances by accessing the network of available life essences for ideas, along with making connections with others to develop new plans.

The Collective Consciousness of mankind is limitless, evolving, and can never end. It is the mind of the energy of the universe, directing the energy functions as it grows and expands. All of mankind has access to the Collective Consciousness and Universal Wisdom through careful attunement and by doing so, can find their life's plan, along with wisdom to live a harmonious life, seek help with answers to questions as they navigate their life, and try to make sense of their life.

Live Your Current Reality

Is there anything holding you back right now? If you wanted to set any goal in your life, or in your career, do you believe you could accomplish it without any hesitation?

My career has not only included work with Laws of the Universe, I have also been an educator and career coach, as it has always been natural for me to want to help others achieve their goals and improve their lives. What I can tell you about the natural answers to those questions is this: a majority of people would answer with a positive response, yet it would also include some type of condition attached to it.

I have met very few people who would feel comfortable believing they could set any goal and just begin to work towards it. Have you heard of an expression, "the struggle is real"? For many people, the struggle is real. I know the natural, human reaction is to think from a limited perspective. If you follow the news, regardless of the format you choose to stay current, you develop an awareness of the scarcity and shortage of many resources in the world. You also become acutely aware of those who are in need, and why should you want for more when there are so many other people who live a disadvantaged life?

But the problem of failing to achieve the goals a person has set, along with the fear of dreaming too big, goes much deeper than just the development of a shortage mindset. Many people just do not know how to bridge the gap between where they are now, and the life they would like to have or thought about living one day. The distance between the two not only seems too great, as a person gets older, it becomes even greater and harder to imagine crossing.

Over time, a person eventually becomes entrenched in the idea of feeling hopeless, frustrated, constrained, restricted, limited, and caught in an endless cycle of hope, belief, and desire - until one day it all turns to unrest and a sense of despair. This is why many people have what is considered to be a mid-life crisis, or why many people later in life just seem to have given up in their dreams, when they no longer believe they can ever reach for their dreams. Their self-doubt has simply taken over their thoughts, and any hope for a better future cannot shine through.

For people who still have a sense of hope, or a belief it is possible to one day have a better life in some manner, these are people who will seek out coaching, mentoring, personal self-development resources, spiritual teachers, and others who may be able to help provide guidance. It is then people learn about living a purpose, developing a dream and creating a vision, living a meaningful life, creating abundance, experiencing ease and a natural flow in their lives, and achieving a sense of renewal. It involves making a transformation from hope and desire, to living and experiencing life with unlimited resources being readily available and feeling a peaceful sense of well-being.

Yet to transform from a life of difficulty to sheer perfection requires a significant change from a personal and spiritual perspective. This is why visualization and thinking thoughts about a new life alone will never change anything. There has to be an energetic shift which occurs from within a person. More importantly, a change can only occur when a person begins to realize they are the reason the change occurs.

This is a difficult lesson for many people to accept, and the reason why many are still trying to figure out how to bridge the gap between a life of struggle and a life of ease. Even as a teacher of Laws of the Universe, I cannot state I have made a complete transformation to a fully perfect state yet, as I am still learning myself. This is the journey I am still on, and as I learn I can share with others to help them learn. It is also possible the journey will not end as lifelong learning is part of continued evolving.

Where I am at in my journey is having learned how to control my thoughts so I can attune to the Collective Consciousness of mankind, readily and easily. This took time and practice, and as I can teach others to accomplish this state of mind, they can learn to do this as well, and they too can reach the wisdom and insight which is readily available for anyone to receive. It is through receiving this knowledge and wisdom I, and anyone who wants to learn, can discover how to bridge the gap between the life lived and the life dreamed about or desired.

This is what I wanted to focus on more as I connected with the Collective Consciousness. I will share with you what I have learned about letting go of self-doubt, to help you bridge the divide between reality and your dreams.

A universal truth is this: Every human being has a perception of the reality they are living now, and this perception can change based upon how well the needs, wants, and desires of the person are being met. But even in an environment which others may be envious of and label perfection, from a perceptual point of view, it may still be viewed as a trap and the worst life possible to another person, if this person feels unfulfilled, incomplete, or unsatisfied in some manner.

This is the nature of reality. Reality is not really real as it can be described in endless ways by humans, as every human has a unique point of view. This point of view can also become laser focused to the point it becomes stuck in one direction. This is what many people would call being hard-headed or opinionated. A person can develop a viewpoint of life and the world and refuse to see it any other way. And so, this is the basis of reality for every human being.

Some of the viewpoints are taught as a child, some learned by the influence of those who surround a person, from childhood through adulthood, along with affiliations chosen as part of a person's life. All of these factors play into and shape how a person sees their reality. Most often people see, feel, and are taught the current reality of life is grim, dire, broken, needs to be fixed, repaired, restored, or any other phrase which may tend to increase feelings of hopelessness about the present.

Many people will look at the current reality, or life around them, and feel a sense of unhappiness. When there is so much negativity surrounding a person, in the news, on the television, or anywhere else, it is a reminder of what is lacking in the world. This may translate into what is lacking in a person's bank account, home, life, career, or anything else personal in nature.

This can happen even if a person has most of what they want out of life. If someone is surrounded by negativity, or taught the world is broken, then this person is going to look for flaws in their own life. This leads to negative feelings.

Now this person will begin to feel frustration, despair, constrained, restrained, held back, limited, and it can all become overwhelming. Then if the person subscribes to some form of inspiration, whether religious, motivational, or therapeutic, there may be some relief felt or experienced on a temporary basis. This creates a cycle of hope, perhaps belief, and then when nothing changes, a return to frustration or worse, despair.

Looking to the Future

With all of this attention placed on the lack of what is desired in a person's life or career in the present, it creates a strong desire or need for future changes. The future is a dream or a vision. It represents living in a fulfilled manner, without any sense of shortage, lack, or limitations, paving the way for a truly meaningful life. The future is the ultimate symbol of hope when reality seems bleak or something is missing now in the present. It represents a new start, a chance to do something different, create a better life, make changes, and have what has been desired for so long. For many people, when they think of the future, it is in terms of what is owed to them, what is needed or wanted, and more importantly, the acquisition of what has been worked towards or earned.

Moving from reality to the future is the promise of hope, a better life, and improved results. The question involves how to get from reality to the desired future. When the future remains a dream, or it doesn't happen quick enough, frustration and negative emotions can set in. The longer this level of unfulfillment is experienced, the more chronic the negative mindset will continue.

When examining the root cause, there are many reasons why the future is so important. While a person may state it has to do with a particular reason, such as a better job, the underlying reason may be a different matter.

Examples of underlying reasons include: Few people live a fully empowered life, which means they decide how they are going to live out each day, unrestricted. The future is an opportunity to change this way of living, or at least it may appear so. Many people want to make up for past mistakes, overcome what they believe is a bad life which has been given to them, or simply escape from everything in the present. The future gives a sense of hope. The fact is, the worse a person's reality may seem now, the more important a future becomes to them.

Seeking Help to Find a New Future

When a person wants to find a way to make the dream of a new future come true, it is possible they will seek help or guidance. Examples of those who may offer help include: In the realm of spirituality self-help, Law of Attraction has become the magic cure or quick fix. It has been taught as the quick jump from reality to the new desired future, through thoughts or visualization. Some teachers may use vague phrases (ready to be ready) to placate followers.

But quick fixes rarely work. And when they don't, followers keep coming back for more, usually receiving the same message again, always hoping it will eventually work. More importantly, when quick fixes do not work, which means a magic jump from reality to the future, it only reinforces the idea of a better life being out of reach or in control by someone or something else.

If a person seeks out motivational speakers or writers, the message may vary from working on the state of mind to the need to face reality. But having to face anything sounds like a person is standing before a firing squad. In other words, it is a negative frame of reference. Others may discuss self-actualization or preparing to find your purpose in life.

These strategies can be helpful, if your mindset is in a positive frame of reference at that time. But if you are desperate to get to a new future, self-improvement isn't going to sit well at this time.

New age teachers may talk about living in the now, which goes to another extreme, by almost tuning out the future. If a person should seek out religious teachers for guidance, they may hear about a divine plan, you "sow what you reap" or getting what is deserved, or to pray for the will of a supreme being to be done for your life.

But how can anyone feel good about their now or later, if it is assigned to them, controlled by someone or something else, or never comes to fruition, which means their life never improves or is realized?

How to Live a Fulfilled Life

Instead of being concerned with how quickly you can get out of the present, and into the future, humans who live fulfilled are those who: *Live Your Current Reality.*

A person is meant to experience life exactly as it is being lived now. What is being felt, should be felt. What a person has or does not have, is exactly as it should be now. There are no mistakes. Living this current reality is part of the process of learning and growing. To be so future focused is to forget the power you possess to gain insight and wisdom. You are not here on this Earth as a human body all on your own. You are part physical body and part energetic form.

Even the human body is comprised of energy itself as it takes living matter and turns it into what appears to be a solid body. The energetic nature of a human occurs through the mind, and this is how every human retains a connection to the Collective Consciousness of mankind. It is through the Collective Consciousness that every human can receive insight from Universal Wisdom. No one is cut off. This is the order of life. And you came into this physical form with a life already planned, knowing in advance how and what you would learn.

How Do You Change Your Focus?

If you have been convinced your reality is too bad, either from what you have heard or what you believe, your future has been the escape plan. It is your ticket out of a troubled life. It will somehow fix the bank account, career, relationship status, or something else. But have you considered how big of a jump that would take to make all at once?

If you follow Law of Attraction teachings: How would you actually visualize or think any of that new future and it just occurs for you? If you wait for God or "the Universe" to act, to make these instant changes: How long must you wait, and do you have to be deemed worthy, follow a certain set of rules, or plead your case?

If you have been focused on a quick fix for so long, and now you are told to live your current reality, could you stop and allow yourself to focus on your present life?

How to Live Your Current Reality

To live your current reality, you need to learn to change your focus. Those who do this as a process of evolving, transforming, and awakening, do so when they finally realize there isn't a supreme being who is controlling their lives, or they no longer have to wait on "the universe" to assist them.

Every person has their own power and it comes from within, through their connection to the energy source of life, and the Collective Consciousness of mankind. The strength of this wisdom is experienced during moments of reflection, meditation, being quiet, sitting in nature, or writing in a journal. This is a time of attuning or listening, changing focus, to gain knowledge and insight necessary to live your present life.

The insight and knowledge received will inspire a person to take action. Some of the action taken will result in the best outcomes, while other outcomes will lead to lessons learned. Either way, it is all part of living the current reality and experiencing life as it was meant to be lived.

Internal Turmoil and Self-Doubt

What causes the internal turmoil for many people, when thinking about the present reality, is wanting it to change but then giving up on their dreams. Your dreams are still very much a part of your life's plan, and those dreams can provide clues about the future direction a person is going. But dreams do not mean a person should live to the point they are solely focused on the future, to the exclusion of the purpose of the present. When the future becomes the driving focus, it can lead to internal turmoil.

There is another type of lived reality for many people, those who have dreamed and then given up, believing it can never happen for them. The underlying cause is usually linked to self-doubt. This is the person who does not believe they are worthy, smart enough, deserving, or capable of receiving their dream. They may have tried and given up. They may lack a positive self-image, prayed and received no answer, visualized and found no changes, or imagined a new life and it never took shape.

Whatever the reason for the doubt, this person believes they are unable to receive the life they want, or they are unable to control their life now. Self-doubt is the reason why many people who are future-focused eventually quit trying, when there are no quick results and the frustration becomes internalized. Self-doubt should actually be labeled learned-doubt. It is a product of what a person comes to believe in life as they have interactions with parents, educational institutions, religious institutions, and others. A person is taught to be dependent on others, especially those in authority, who can have a direct impact on a person's life and how they live. When a person wants to think for themselves, it creates a spark of doubt.

Doubt is reinforced in the workplace as well, where the team effort is emphasized and management rules. No matter what creates the internalized doubt, self-doubt is not a natural state, and learning about the underlying Laws of the Universe can help to explain why. Those who seek to learn can discover knowledge through their own mind, as every human is and will always be connected to the energy source of life. A teacher can also assist, one who is willing to share truths and laws as knowledge, not quick fixes.

Learn a Law of the Universe

One Universal Law which can help to broaden a person's understanding of their connection to the Collective Consciousness of mankind, and the power available to live in and experience the present reality, is the Law of Singularity.

The Law of Singularity states: *A single focus creates a well-defined purpose, and a single energy stream creates life.*

Mankind has used this Universal Law in other ways, specifically to create power. For example, stating there is "one true God", a supreme being, establishing a dictator, and a religious leader. It is even found in relationships and the term monogamous relationships.

But from an energetic perspective, this Law of the Universe is related to the purpose a human being has while in a physical form. Each person made their own life's plan, and agreements with others if there were to be outcomes co-produced together. But each person has a body which operates independently, thinks on its own, and the very energetic essence of the body is all its own. All of your memories are yours alone, and retained in Collective Consciousness, even after the physical form is gone.

This is an example of how Laws of the Universe underpin all of life. You live singularly, your body functions singularly, you access the source of life singularly, which means independence is natural. Dependence and doubt are learned.

This Law of the Universe is your power to live your life as you want it, which means you can live now and experience your reality in peace. When you have a dream of the future, it is something you have planned and are working towards. It should be a source of inspiration rather than escape. The plan every human creates for their life is flexible to some degree. It can accelerate if a person is focused on a well-defined purpose or living the Law of Singularity. Or if it can slow if a person is frustrated by only focusing on the future to escape the present.

The Most Import Lesson of All

The most important lesson any human can learn is this: Your Future is Now.

There is so much going on right now in a person's life which is vital to their becoming, to ignore it is to miss out on essential learning opportunities. A person does not reach the future by jumping ahead, or visualizing and magically getting there, there is a process of becoming which every human goes through.

More importantly, there is no future. There is only now.

There is either living or returning to an energetic form. Instead of stating: "I want something in the future", just state: "My goal is to complete something". Then you have a specific and concrete goal or purpose, and you can develop an action plan to build from along the way.

For those who use Law of Attraction alone, ask yourself this question: How can you create a vision of the future when you have no idea who you will have become by then?

What is most important is that you live and experience today.

Even the worst possible circumstances you might image are all part of your being and becoming. As you focus on the present, you develop a better mindset, and then you can listen for the insight and guidance needed. Through any form of reflection, you will receive insight and knowledge from the Collective Consciousness and Universal Wisdom of mankind, helping you become empowered and living at peace. Then you can set goals, and as you dream, look for clues about the plan for your life.

You can have the most amazing life you have ever imagined, and it all starts now.

CHAPTER 4.
LAWS OF THE UNIVERSE

Over the past few years, there is one Law of the Universe which has become well-known and it is Law of Attraction. One of the challenges for the current popularity of Law of Attraction, is a matter of how it is being taught. This universal law is being taught as if it is the only Law of the Universe, which is misleading for the many followers who attempt to implement it in the manner provided by the Law of Attraction teachers.

This was the case for me, and why I eventually outgrew the Law of Attraction teachers. I tried to live my life just by implementing Law of Attraction and found that while I could begin a personal transformation, this alone was not enough to answer all of the questions I had or bring about the results described by the teachers of Law of Attraction. More importantly, I could feel there were other laws these teachers were not explaining.

As I began to look beyond Law of Attraction, I discovered there are a generally accepted set of 12 universal laws, although I am not certain I understand how these laws were decided upon or by whom. These universal laws attempt to explain how the universe operates and include: Law of Divine Oneness, Law of Vibration, Law of Action, Law of Correspondence, Law of Cause and Effect, Law of Compensation, Law of Attraction, Law of Perpetual Transmutation of Energy, Law of Relativity, Law of Polarity, Law of Rhythm, and Law of Gender.

I did not set out to learn these laws as I discovered my natural ability to attune to Collective Consciousness and higher order Universal Wisdom, and this is what I wanted to devote my time to developing. I also discovered as I sought out Universal

Wisdom, I could learn other Laws of the Universe - laws that were not included in the list described above. This told me I should keep an open mind and not conform to someone else's view of how the universe operates, and instead, be open to what I was receiving from Universal Wisdom.

As I continued my journey and improved my ability to attune my thoughts, I began gaining better clarity about the many Laws of the Universe. What you will learn about in this chapter are just a few of the many of the Laws of the Universe.

Accessing Universal Wisdom

I have an ability to access to Collective Consciousness and Universal Wisdom, just as every living person does, as we are all part of the source of life, and we are all connected to and sustain the energy of the universe. I have been aware of my ability to easily access the source of life energy from a very early age. For a long time, I viewed it as something which made me different, then as something which makes me unique. But now I see this not as a gift, but I see myself as someone who has a unique ability to listen, and listen at a profoundly deep and intuitive level, and do so in a manner which allows me to hear beyond my own thoughts.

This also does not require receiving a special appointment by a supreme being or source, rather it only requires I find the inner harmonious connection to the source of life which resides in all of us. Too many people have cut this connection off by believing there is someone or something else in charge of the universe, someone they must appease or make happy, and follow a prescribed set of rules to find their way to happiness in life.

I never believed in this dogma and I am not certain I know why. Perhaps I came into life with a fierce determination to be a teacher and never doubt my inner guidance, although it took me over 40 years to trust it and nurture it. But here I am now, ready to follow this pathway where ever this may take me, and willing to help others in whatever manner I believe will be of the most benefit.

I will share the Laws of the Universe I have learned about to date, while connected to Universal Wisdom through quiet meditation and focused attention.

Law of Connection: Forming Attachments

Do you wonder how it is you feel automatically drawn to someone else, as if you have known them your entire life? Do you ever wonder how it is you seem to feel a connection with someone you barely know? Is it possible every human is connected to a consciousness, referred to by some as the eternal soul, and others as Infinite Intelligence? Would you like to better understand the connection between humans, from a spiritual or metaphysical perspective?

One of the most popular Laws of the Universe is Law of Attraction. What most people are not taught by the Law of Attraction teachers, and/or do not understand while attempting to apply it to their lives, is that Law of Attraction cannot act alone. Why? In order to attract someone into your life, you must first make a connection with this person, whether at a conscious or subconscious level.

A conscious connection is one which can be immediately recognized and acknowledged, usually cultivated over time and through life experiences. A subconscious connection is one which may be felt rather than immediately recognized, one that is experienced through emotional reactions.

Connection to the Energy of Life

All humans have an unending and limitless connection to the energy of life, along with the Collective Consciousness of mankind. This is called the Law of Connection.

A connection to the source of life energy means the dynamic balance of positive and negative energy exists. A person can be attuned to positive or negative energy. Whatever your mental tuner is focused on, or your thoughts, attraction brings more from that flow of energy: positive or negative.

A person who lives through reflections on the past, they develop a focus that attracts more of the same, which is usually negative energy. Negative energy is where the past resides as it contains hurt, regret, bad feelings, loss, and pain. Positive energy is joy, love, acceptance, forgiving, and feelings of hope. And while the past can contain positive memories, the negative memories often outweigh the positive memories.

As with any spectrum, there is a midpoint, a balance in the middle of positive and negative. That is a time referred to as quieting the mind during meditation. It also occurs during sleep as the mind is no longer attuned to one energy spectrum and thoughts subside. Sleep can perform a reset for the mental tuner. However, people who have a practiced pattern of thought, a chronic focus on negativity, it will take more than sleep to change that focus. It will now require a conscious, steady focus on positivity to shift attention.

A Universal Truth: Energy requires life for sustenance.

Just as energy produces life, life is needed to sustain energy. Energy needs input to keep it in motion and flowing. From that flow comes life, and life creates several points of output, in order for energy to flow outward and create manifestations. Some manifestations are thoughts or what is referred to as the intangible. Other manifestations are the tangible or the physical.

All life adds to and creates energy. The animals are the positive realm and sustain that current. Humans fluctuate and provide negative energy that is vital or necessary to keep a constant state of flux. Both positive and negative currents create the whole known as energy.

Animals are always attuned to the energy of life and never stray from the positive current. Some animals remain "untamed" as they serve a purpose for sustaining forests, serving as a food source, or maintain balance with the energy flow. Animals who grow close to humans are easy to adore and appreciate because of their calm state of being.

Humans have a different frequency and can maintain a positive or negative focus based upon the purpose they have chosen. Some have chosen to experience an existence of what is called pleasure or pain or upheaval or ease or uncertainty or free-flowing. When a human being sees another who is suffering, they express their discomfort through pity or an offer to help. But that pain, that very existence they chose, provides sustenance to the source of life energy.

Humans who are creative are those who can discern the flow of energy and attract a stream of like-minded thoughts or consciousness. A writer taps into streams of ideas and collects thoughts. An artist taps into imagery. All of this, every piece of writing or art, are manifestations that add to and cause energy to expand, given by the existence of humans and animals. No matter what a person chooses to believe about their existence, they are connected to, contribute to, sustain, and are sustained by the source of life energy.

Law of Connection

The connection to the energy of life creates the foundation for the Law of Connection. A life essence, while part of the Collective Consciousness and not yet in physical form here on Earth, may decide to develop a life plan and pre-arrange connections with others for the time here in physical form. This explains the feeling of knowing someone from past lives, or somehow having found your soulmate as you feel a seemingly unexplainable instantaneous connection. The pre-arranged connections may not only be made with people, but also with places and events, which would explain the feeling of déjà vu.

The Law of Connection also relates to the manner in which people connect with and relate to each other in general. This is how Law of Attraction works in conjunction with Law of Connection. When a person is focused on or attuned to the negative energy spectrum, they are likely to only attract someone else who is also focused on the same energy spectrum. For example, if a person is focused on negative feelings of depression, they will likely attract someone who is also focused on negative emotions as well. The converse is also true concerning positive emotions and attracting someone who is also focused on the positive energy spectrum.

The Law of Connection allows human beings to form attachments with each other, and retain memories developed even after the physical forms are gone. The Law of Connection allows memories, emotions, and feelings to form a neural network between humans, which is retained in the minds of those who have connected, and it is stored in the limitless Collective Consciousness for access and retrieval.

Law of Connection: Forming Attachments Summary

The nature of energy is fluid, moving, living, and it is accessible through connection points. As an example, energy is harnessed through power lines. Something accesses the energy, yet the connection does not have to be permanent. An appliance makes a connection and has the energy or power necessary to function but does not need it permanently unless required or programmed. The appliance can also run on energy by accessing any connection point or compatible outlet. The energy itself does not remember the appliance or retain a memory of its connection.

<u>Humans are Energy</u>: Part physical form (which is still energetic at its core) and energetic by being connected through the mind to the source of life energy.

<u>Human to Human Connections</u>: It is an energy to energy connection, which is a relationship, with energy engaged at a connection point. A relationship can last for a few minutes or several lifetimes, depending upon the intention, agreements, and life plans.

From a connection point, Law of Connection states the attachment is a result of energetic memories created while two or more beings act together. The connection point is held as strong as the intention, which humans experience as feelings and emotions. For example: It is called love when an intention is to bond or sadness when a connection ends.

An Example of a Human to Human Connection:

Human A (Part Physical Form, Energetic Being) - Who has a connection through the mind to the energy source of life. The mind also remembers pasts events and it is perceptual in nature, which means the manner in which this person remembers an event, situation, or set of circumstances can be different from someone else.

Human B (Part Physical Form, Energetic Being) - Who has a connection through the mind to the energy source of life. The mind also remembers pasts events and it is perceptual in nature, which means the manner in which this person remembers an event, situation, or set of circumstances can be different from someone else.

As memories are created, positive memories are stored within the positive energy spectrum of the Collective Consciousness of mankind and negative memories are stored within the negative energy spectrum. The neutral area of Collective Consciousness, where positive and negative energy spectrums meet, stores the life plans of humans. All lessons learned, insight gained, or wisdom acquired from life is stored in higher order Universal Wisdom.

Connection Between Human A and Human B: This occurs through the mind and is felt or experienced as emotions. It transpires at an energetic level and is facilitated by intentions, an agreement, and life plans. The connection point is where the two have made the physical and energetic connection. In modern society, an online dating website might facilitate romantic connections which can be short-term or long-term in nature.

This connection creates another energy stream but it does not transmit or receive signals from Collective Consciousness, only the minds of humans. This is why two people who are in a relationship, which is a connection, often feel as if they are attuned to each other and sense what the other one is experiencing or feeling. They have created a new energy stream together and through their minds they are transmitting and receiving energy.

Law of Attunement: Changing Your Focus and Vibration

What gets most of your time and attention? What do you focus on during the day? Do you tend to let your mind wander or jump from one thought to the next? Can you easily attune to positive feelings if you decide you want to do so, especially if you experience negative emotions?

Every day human beings experience visual stimulation and it is increasing at a rate that it is easy to become over-stimulated. This is a technology-based society and more than ever there are devices and apps trying to gain attention of a human's mind and attention. Some people are better able to clearly focus when there is so much demand for their attention, while many others struggle to concentrate - especially while on the job.

A Universal Truth: Energy has no expiration date and never ends.

Animals and humans have what is referred to as an expiration date. It depends upon their chosen purpose and design. All creatures have a defined time, no matter how sudden or seemingly random their departure may be.

Energy would only cease to exist if there was nothing left to sustain it and that would not occur unless every planet and every galaxy were to be removed from existence, and that could never be. Energy naturally produces new life and new manifestations, a cycle that causes the source energy to expand exponentially.

Law of Attunement

Much has been spoken and written about the Laws of the Universe, specifically, Law of Attraction, as it seems to provide the easiest answers for those in need. The fact is that the answers sought are not a result of applying a single Law of the Universe, but a collective set of laws. One law of significant importance for those seeking answers, and those who find they are out of alignment, is the Law of Attunement.

Anyone can attune. Everyone attunes to some degree by default, and it is often referred to as focus. Attunement can be shallow or cursory, or a complete connection to what is called Infinite Intelligence, God, Source, or a Collective Consciousness.

The writer of this book can quickly attune to the highest frequency - even in unusual settings, or noisy places for a brief time. The strongest connection occurs in a peaceful environment with prompts such as ambient music. This higher connection has been felt for many years and allowed to cultivate over time. At first there was a natural fear about what was being experienced. Acceptance grew as the writer began to better understand energy and how easily he could feel, see, sense, and experience energy all around him.

Attunement and Control

But just like a radio, this connection can be turned off and attention placed on other matters. It is always a choice. What the writer now understands is that flourishing requires attunement. By default, everyone attunes to personal interests and desires. Some pray, wish, hope, and fervently plead to some unknown source to change their lives, without realizing they have control. The control they have available is not action, it is attunement.

If a person decides to attune, they can change their focus, vibration, and flow of energy to a positive source, and take full advantage of Collective Consciousness. Most people choose split energy: both negative and positive. This means a person is frequently changing moods, experiencing a wide range of emotions during day based upon current circumstances. It is often reactive in nature, which is the reason why emotional intelligence has become such a widely discussed topic now.

People are so often over-stimulated and unable to control their emotions and feelings that an entire intelligence type has been identified as being in need of development.

As much has been written about emotional intelligence, it would seem people could easily control their feelings. But this isn't always the case and why the topic seems to remain so popular. Despite knowing the importance of maintaining control of one's emotions, along with the reactions to what one is feeling, many people cannot seem to retain this state of being. Why? It is a matter of not knowing how to attune.

Attunement requires calm. It does not mean that the "little voices of doubt" or the negative energy experienced will cease to exist, as it cannot cease to exist. But attunement means directing your attention to the calm place inside your mind, where inspiration, guidance, and wisdom will arrive. It is a matter of recognizing which of the energy spectrums you are focused on and making a conscious decision to change your point of focus.

For example, if you are experiencing negative circumstances in your work environment, this does not automatically create within you a negative response. But if you use those circumstances to then reflect upon past negative events and remain attuned to negative energy, you will be focused on negative feelings and emotions.

If you are focused or attuned to negative emotions, this is not the time to take action or respond to circumstances. You will know when it is time to take action when you have received insight and wisdom, as it will feel fresh, exciting, and new. The writer of this book is building the pages of this book as a beacon, or a source of knowledge, and a powerful holder of energy to those who want to learn to facilitate attunement. The more practiced a person can become with attuning to positive energy, the easier it will be for them to find the wisdom needed from Collective Consciousness to live their life and discover their life's plan.

Law of Attunement: Changing Your Focus and Vibration Summary

<u>The Law of Attunement states</u>: A mind which is fully attuned to its highest state has done so when full control of the conscious and subconscious processes have been achieved.

<u>The Human Mind</u>: It is a processing center of energy, information, and senses. There are automatic functions, subconscious activities, energetic functioning, conscious input, and processing from the senses. A daily life is filled with hundreds upon hundreds of auditory, visual, and tactile inputs from the senses to process.

<u>Focus, Attention Span, Concentration</u>: These are words used to describe an ability to concentrate on a specific topic, task, or subject. However, other mental processes still continue, such as automatic and energetic processes and functions. The mind is also connected to energetic levels, and it has access to past occurrences and future plans.

One form of focused thinking is the highest level of control, taking command of the mind to purposely seek higher knowledge and wisdom. This is called *attuning* or being able to control almost every mental function to the point there is a single focus on asking questions and receiving answers. All other thoughts are tuned out, all sensory input is minimized, and command of the mind has begun. Most people struggle to learn to do this, even with practice, as society is sensory driven.

In addition, religion teaches the use of prayers, which are cursory deposits of wishes, requiring minimal effort and little focus attention or effort. Those who attune well often have some form of meditative practice. This could include meditation, yoga, journaling, writing, some forms of introspective praying, hiking, walking, gardening, cooking, household repairs, ore anything else which allows a person to look within, calm their mind, gain control, and seek higher knowledge.

Usually teachers are the ones who have mastered this practice, yet to be a great teacher requires a commitment to practice and develop mastery of the chosen craft. The longer a person practices attunement, the strong they become, until one day they can live a life plugged in at any given time. This means at any moment this person can change their point of focus and vibration and be immediately available to receive knowledge and insight from the Collective Consciousness of mankind, along with higher order Universal Wisdom. It also means the person will go further in their quest for knowledge and wisdom of mankind. It is this practice of attuning which I have accomplished and continue to master as a teacher of the Laws of the Universe.

Law of Interaction: Internal and External Interactions

Have you considered how your mind, the very essence of your being, is able to interact with your environment while also connected to the Collective Consciousness of mankind? While the human body may have limitations, and it may seem as if the brain is limited because it is restricted to a particular size and shape, the mind is limitless. Human beings cannot comprehend the nature of the mind because it so complex. It is able to transmit and receive signals and vibrations simultaneously, and without the intentional direction of the human's conscious thoughts itself. The mind is connected to the Collective Consciousness and the body at the same time, as a result of Law of Interaction.

A Universal Truth: Everything there is in existence, everything that was created, everything that will be made or thought or written, is done because of the Law of Interaction.

<u>The Law of Interaction states</u>: Energy is sustained by the interaction of positive and negative streams.Higher order Universal Wisdom, retained in Collective Consciousness, is sustained with the interaction of human minds sending and transmitting signals with wisdom, insight, and knowledge, along with requests made for guidance.

Collective Consciousness is sustained by the interaction of energy flowing to and from the human mind, through impulses or signals which transmit new memories, ideas, words, images, and all thought forms generated by human beings.

Examples of Law of Interaction: New writings, music, paintings, drawings, ideas, inspiration, insight, and much more are a result of the interaction of a mind willing to tap into insight, creativity, and knowledge - with the source of all that being higher order Universal Wisdom. This interaction may become so practiced that the ideas flow naturally and easily, to the point a person just has to focus briefly and receive wisdom.

Some people tap into this interactive state not really understanding the process but knowing it works as they have seen the results. Others may give it a name or attribute it to a divine cause. But everything is a result of an energetic state, an interaction of the signals which the mind transmits.

The mind is always producing thoughts and some of those thoughts interact with past memories, tapping into one end of the energy spectrum. Some thoughts are processing events of the day and that is often when inspiration comes through, when there are fewer filters ready to block it out or hide it.

Daily Interactions

The Law of Interaction teaches we cannot live without interacting. We wake up and interact with our environment. We interact with others. But the most important interactions are those in our mind. If we allow our mind to just wander, and thoughts to change from one subject to the next without purpose, we are missing out on important interactions with Collective Consciousness and higher order Universal Wisdom.

There are answers to life we all seek, we all want wisdom of some kind, or at least direction of some variety. This is evident in those who pray. When a person's mind is active and focused, they have an opportunity to interact with Collective Consciousness in a purposeful manner. This form of interaction can be done through controlled and focused thinking, which sends out signals seeking knowledge and wisdom. It allows the needed insight to be transmitted to the person requesting it. The Law of Interaction can occur naturally or without having to request it, and it can also occur as a focused process.

The Law of Interaction also has a direct bearing on how humans get along as they are fact to face. When two people are speaking to each other, it is still an energetic process with humans sending or transmitting signals. While you are involved in a physical or human interaction, it is still possible to receive guidance from Collective Consciousness and higher order Universal Wisdom. This requires focus, calm, and intent.

It then becomes a matter of interacting on a physical level and paying attention to that interaction, while also being open and receptive to receiving insight from higher order Universal Wisdom. It is possible for a human mind to be interacting from two perspectives, as long as you are poised, calm, focused, and carefully listening.

Law of Interaction: Internal and External Interactions Summary

<u>A Human, Energetic Being interacts with another Human, Energetic Being/Beings</u>: The interaction may take place in the form of a look, comments while passing by, a phone call, a purchase made in a store, a visual connection, an auditory exchange, physical interaction, or any other number of possible interaction types.

An interaction is a temporary energetic exchange. For example, with communication or an external interaction, the sender uses energy to develop a message to be communicated. There is a thought and it will be spoken to the receiver. The receiver uses energy to receive and process the communicated message. The message is heard and a response made. However, the interaction (in the form of communication) is not always a two-way process as the receiver may not chose to respond or act/react when the message is received from the sender.

There are internal interactions which occur when information, data, and sensory input is received. A person will think and then do something, or think and then act, or process the information and respond. It is also a temporary energetic process, but it is not an exchange as another person or persons are not involved.

The Law of Interaction states: At the basis of all interactions between human beings is the need to influence another, through words spoken or actions taken.

Example of Interactions:

A person states to another person: Today is Friday. This is an auditory statement. The point of influence is the person's knowledge of the days of the week.

A person calls someone and asks if they are available to help with a move. This is another auditory interaction. The point of influence is gaining this person's assistance.

A person looks at someone and smiles directly at this person. This is a visual interaction. The point of influence is to create a feeling of warmth within the receiver of the message.

A person engages in sex with another person. This is a physical interaction. The point of influence is creating, engaging in, and obtaining feelings of pleasure, eroticism, and sexual gratification.

When people write about improving the process of communication, it is often done from the perspective of the sender understanding the needs and wants of the receiver. What helps more than this knowledge is understanding how interactions involve influence and that it occurs at an energetic level.

To interact with someone means you are going to establish a connection, which is energetic in nature, even if it is only temporary. Once connected, the interaction takes place, with an attempt to influence the other person's actions.

A modern example: An online dating website has facilitated a connection between two people who have met and connected. The form of the interaction was physical as a sexual encounter occurred. One person influenced the other or made a "first move" towards satisfying feelings of sexual pleasure. Other interactions may also occur, such as conversations, as each person attempts to share their best attributes and work to build a long-term connection. This demonstrates how multiple Laws of the Universe are at work.

Law of Intention: Creating Your Own Life

Would you like to know the source of true happiness and fulfillment in your life? Would you be surprised if you found out: How your life plays out is a direct result of your actions, which means you are in control and no one else? I challenge you to consider this as I share with you what I have learned.

I have been on a journey my entire life, although I was not fully aware of the impact of this journey until recently. I now realize I was naturally able to listen to the connection which all humans have to the energy source we are part of and give life to, from a very early age. I also realize now that I am naturally able to listen to the Collective Consciousness and higher order Universal Wisdom, because I would never accept that I was separated from it by someone or something else. While I did not understand what any of that really meant until now, I knew it instinctually and I experienced it naturally.

Law of Intention: When you can accept control of your life, when you can understand your connection to the source of life energy, and you can live according to the Law of Intention. The Law of Intention states your purpose is defined by what you intend to create with your life, and how you focus your thoughts and actions.

Here are common scenarios and why humans are not aware of the Law of Intention:

Scenario Number One: Belonging to a religious viewpoint

A person goes to church or subscribes to a religious belief that tells them they must follow specific rules and guidelines. Then if this person has met and qualified for special treatment, their prayers will be answered. Sometimes they must repent for their past and vow to never live like that again, determined never to anger the supreme being who controls all of mankind and the universe.

This means the only control they have is over their ability to follow the right rules. The problem is that the rules can vary from one religious group to another, and that is why there are wars in the name of a supreme being. It is not possible for everyone to agree upon who or what this supreme being may be and how much control this being has since it is a representation of the actual truth; and both wars or fights are meant to prove the other group is wrong, as if one group has absolute proof.

That is what happens at a group or religious level. What about at an individual level?

A person tries to live according to the rules, believing they live according to what someone else intends. It is external based control, by someone or something else. When a person decides to reject the very idea of what religions taught, they may break some or all of the rules; both of religion and of society. Those who are in jail are often the ones who are shouting the loudest against a system of controls.

People who reject the idea of having to live according to what someone else, or some other religious group, or some supreme being intends, may seek out alternative forms of what is called spirituality. This is how many have followed the rise of the teachings of the Law of Attraction.

Scenario Number Two: Following Law of Attraction

Law of Attraction is the other scenario and why so many people are unaware of the Law of Intention, along with other Laws of the Universe. Law of Attraction seems like a quick way to draw followers to teachers, especially those who are deeply dissatisfied with and unable to connect to traditional religious teachings. It allows teachers to create dependency as Law of Attraction only resolves some of the questions being asked.

Law of Attraction can be helpful, as a starting point in a person's journey, as this author has discovered, but it also used by itself can still create a sense of someone or something else being in charge. For example, one teacher uses words that include source energy and the vortex. These words give the impression there is a universal team who can provide assistance if you have the right state of mind. But again, that is not the complete answer. Law of Attraction is called upon, not relied upon, as part of fulfilling a person's life.

Living Law of Intention

To understand Law of Intention, you must be willing to accept you are part of the source of life, you are connected to the energy of life, you are part of Collective Consciousness, and you have access to Universal Wisdom. There is no luck, magic, or supreme being in charge. There is no team made up in energy who is waiting to do your bidding or create the life of your dreams. You are in charge.

When you accept that you have control, you can allow Law of Intention to work. Focus clearly on your life and what you want it to be. Establish clarity and be prepared to listen and look for insight from Universal Wisdom. Your powerful intention draws to you those people, places, and things that will create and manifest what is part of your life's plan.

You must be focused on the positive energy spectrum, with happiness and hope, to receive the strongest signals and vibrations, and develop the widest open possible connection to Universal Wisdom. This is your life, you are the source of life.

Law of Intention: Creating Your Own Life Summary

The Law of Intention states: The true intention of a human begins at an energetic level, regardless of the words spoken, which is a product of thoughts and other mental activities.

The following is a practical example: A personal makes a statement to another person: "I am going on, or I intend to go on, a diet today." The intention has been stated.

From an energetic perspective, this person has already thought about the many attempts to diet and how each one failed. What this person actually intends to do is to start and stop as soon as the supply of salads in the refrigerator runs out. This person has no intention of trying to attempt a diet again given the past failure rate. Anyone who knows this person well or has a strong connection with him/her (which means having an energetic connection) may likely have picked upon on the true intention already.

What a person intends to do with their life: Early on in a person's life there may be more choices available. A person may choose a career, decide when to form relationships, decide upon a job or jobs, and make a decision as to where to live. What there will always be felt from within is some desire of what is wanted, whether or not it is ever completely fulfilled. This is at an energetic level and based upon a person's life plan.

Yet what is felt at an energetic level often comes into conflict with what is thought about as societal roles and responsibilities dictate what a person should be doing. The true intention held comes into conflict with expectations. When expectations and responsibilities overshadow a person's life, it becomes the dominating or driving force which guides their daily actions.

Now a person who has never fulfilled their true intention, they will call it a dream and refer to it as something to be done in the future. Then when this true intention, that which a person really wants to do with their life, can no longer be ignored as it exists at an energetic level, they will refer to it as a calling. Many will call it a time of finding their true north or doing what they are most passionate about in life. But in reality, this person has decided they will no longer allow responsibilities and roles to be the deciding factors for how they live their life. It is then they will move towards living what has always existed at an energetic level.

Law of Clarity: Understanding the Purpose of Challenges

Have you experienced loss, or know of someone who suffered what seemed to be an unexplainable loss? I certainly have in my life. I lost my father several years ago in a car accident and the nature of it was unexplainable to me. I could not comprehend why this had occurred. It happened at a time when I was on my journey of understanding the laws of the universe, or at least beginning to understand the basics. I had been searching my entire life to understand this internal connection to something I felt, and the disconnection to organized religion I could not explain.

By the time of the car accident, I had been studying teachers of Law of Attraction for approximately three years, and these teachings were helpful to an extent with the initial feelings I experienced about the loss. However, the primary teacher of Law of Attraction, who I have followed until recently, states that there is no death experience and always seemed to talk around the subject of death, rather than talk about it. I never received any answers about this subject, and I listened to other teachers. It seemed that Law of Attraction teachers could not fully address the subject of death.

I understand the concept of eternal energy, and I know we are connected as humans, which means I can connect to the energy of my father through focused thought. But to me, this still does not explain the event of losing him in the first place. I set the question aside until recently, when I heard of a tragic story involving parents who lost a newborn.

This baby had a brain tumor and struggled from the time of birth, through an extensive operation, and attempt to survive, only to lose its life. I could see and sense the anguish the parents experienced. This reawakened the question I have held for so long about the purpose of tragedy. This question led me to search for answers. I will share with you what I have learned, to help you if you have experienced such a loss.

A universal truth is this: Mankind is driven to excel, to innovate, to create, and reach for greater wisdom while faced with challenges and problems.

This is a problem-based existence. Every great invention, all progress, all innovation, all evolution in society and throughout time, is the result of problems and challenges. If these challenges did not exist, man would not need a reason to look within to question, to explore, to search, to seek out answers, to understand, to fight, to solve, or to change whatever they believe is the cause of the problem.

Many of the challenges and problems that present itself to mankind are the result of human's existence, growth, progress, and other related factors. Some problems and challenges are natural and related to the elements of the universe, which are also planned according to the greater needs of man, according to the Universal Wisdom of man, and what is needed to balance the energy of the universe.

Some of the problems and challenges faced by humans are individual in nature rather than something a collective society must address. The individual challenges and problems can set the course for a man or woman, determine who they are or will become, guide their life, shape their future, and create their ultimate destiny.

Being Challenge Focused

Mankind is problem and challenge focused. Problems and challenges are necessary if a man or woman wants to experience their fullness, if they want to come into their own, if they want to learn of their very essence, and know who they really are as a person. The problem for most people, related to challenge, is the negative connotation associated with the very idea that someone has been faced with a problem.

When a person has a series of challenges, they may call it being under a dark cloud. The label depression has been given to people who cannot accept the power they have to control and resolve their own problems. This is often due to religious teachings and a feeling of external control for what happens to a person's life. When there is a problem, people are taught to pray. Then if they have met the right conditions, served penance, did not anger the supreme being, and followed the right set of rules, they will likely receive help with their problem.

The Big Challenges

Then there are people who love the idea of battling big challenges so they can state that they fought and won, they survived, and proclaim their victory to the world, believing it will inspire others as well. They form groups, have assigned or designated colors, announce their victories, and seek to achieve great recognition in public for their valiant efforts of conquering this challenge or series of challenges.

But at the heart of all of this is an individual process. Man or woman is faced with a problem or challenge, and then they must choose, or not choose, to address it. As part of being a problem-based existence, it is possible for a man or woman to purposely introduce problems and challenges, to prompt innovation, change, progress, and forward thinking or creativity. Sometimes this is done as part of a life's journey, and sometimes it is preplanned.

Seeing the Bigger Picture

Those who are awakening to the universal laws and truths begin to accept and understand: Mankind is part of the source of life and endless energy; A physical existence is merely a physical form added to energy already in existence; and They are in control and no one else.

What this means for mankind is that an existence on Earth, in physical form, is already preplanned; not by a supreme being, but by the essence of energy that is man. This plan for existence on Earth can be amended to some degree once a person is here, but the plan remains intact. This plan includes details about challenges and problems which will be included at certain points to help prompt growth, leading to times of self-discovery.

The Challenge of Loss

One of these problems or challenges is facing loss. Every person connected to a man or a woman's existence is part of a plan. Their timing is known ahead of time, their involvement was agreed upon, and the length of time in the person's life is known at a subconscious or energetic level, whether the time period is long or short, pleasant or disturbing. This includes the arrival and exit of these people in and out of a person's life.

What creates a unique challenge for a man or a woman is sudden loss, especially when it is a seemingly random, senseless, tragic, violent, unplanned, or other similar type of loss; and the person lost was of particular significance. It may be difficult to imagine this type of loss could ever fulfill or serve a purpose.

For those who experience this type of loss, they may not move forward from it, and this challenge may keep them trapped in that moment in time indefinitely. But there will be an eventual time of clarity, when emotions subside, and wisdom flows through to the person. A deeply held religious perspective can either prolong the resistance or help to calm a person down, depending upon their choice of words. When a person states they have faith, it means they have a belief in a purpose, whether or not they are yet willing to listen and hear it.

At some point a person will allow Universal Wisdom to flow through, even if gradually, and the plan or purpose will begin to become realized, even if the man or woman never fully understands it. All relationships have purpose and meaning. The timing of all relationships was made as part of the life created while deciding on a physical existence for Earth. The timing includes the arrival and exit dates of these relationships. All has meaning and purpose, and all is in your control as part of the energy of life.

Understanding Loss

When a person has experienced a loss of someone they cared about, from one of their relationships, it can be difficult to see its purpose or understand how it could be part of a plan. That is why it is important to listen for Universal Wisdom to help guide you past your emotions, to show you how this challenge was meant to help you, and how it was part of your plan to begin with in some manner.

At its very essence, a deeply emotional challenge can cause a person to look within and rediscover who they are. It can cause an awakening to one's true self. This challenge can also draw a person closer to their mate and create a bond, which provides unity and strength. The loss might also lead to prompting a bigger purpose, such as helping others with a similar situation, depending upon the type of loss or circumstances surrounding it, even leading to changes in society.

You as part of the source of life energy, part of the creator of life, developed a unique plan for your life. When you discover your purpose, which may come about through challenges and problems that have been preplanned, you will find not only your personal strength, you will discover your true personal power and connection to the energy which creates all of life and is nurtured by mankind's existence.

Law of Clarity: Understanding the Purpose of Challenges Summary

The Law of Clarity states: Clarification of the mind occurs first at an energetic level, when any human is seeking answers or to understand that which they cannot easily or readily comprehend when faced with challenges.

The following is an example: A person seeks clarification, to understand the purpose of a recent job loss. This job loss is challenging from many aspects, including financial and psychological. This person cannot immediately find answers as to why the job loss occurred or why it was necessary. The Law of Clarity indicates the clarification will come first at an energetic level.

This occurs over time, as a person is able to reflect and look beyond the incident. This is a challenge-oriented society and humans are also challenge-oriented, which means challenges produce learning opportunities. Through moments of reflection, such as thinking, writing, walking, or doing anything to switch mindsets, a person can receive clarification through insight and wisdom received from the Collective Consciousness.

This can also apply to other examples:

A person who lost a loved one and it was unexpected or tragic. The circumstances will cause the time it takes to reach a reflection point to vary. The more extreme the circumstances, the longer it may take.

A person who does not feel they fit into society and now it seems as if they are never going to achieve anything in life.

True Clarification

True clarification must come through a person's energetic essence as this is where the connection to Collective Consciousness is experienced. During periods of challenge, or times immediately afterwards, a person's mind will be filled with thoughts of the incident, imagined scenarios, and this person will be experiencing many emotional reactions.

At the core of a person, which is their energetic essence, insight and wisdom is available. This wisdom may include details about the purpose of the challenge, from the perspective of the greater life purpose, and/or insight into the life plan this person has already created. Clarification is available at any time, whenever a person is ready to reflect, mediate, turn within, or listen for inner wisdom. It is also available to anyone and everyone as no one is cut off from the Collective Consciousness of mankind.

Law of Presence: Fulfilling Your Purpose

Would you like to know how you can make your mark in this world? Are you interested in learning how you can cause your voice to be heard, one person and one voice among millions of others in the world?

This is something I have been considering as I have been thinking about my career as an educator in the field of academia, and an aspiring teacher of the Laws of the Universe.

As an aspiring teacher of Laws of the Universe, this came about after following teachers of Law of Attraction and not having my questions answered. A turning point for me came about when I went on a cruise in 2017 with one of the prominent Law of Attraction teachers and it was the same message presented I've heard for many years, the same questions being asked by her followers, and it felt as if dependency was being taught, not truths being shared by this teacher.

I believed if Laws of the Universe were taught, many of these followers, myself included, would find their awakening. But listening to this teacher did push me along until I finally realized there were more answers to be found.

Yet I felt some hesitancy as I know there are many Law of Attraction teachers and this is a field which may be viewed in a skeptical light, especially by those with a strong religious upbringing. I wondered how I would convince people I was not making this knowledge up or stating something about the universe which was untrue.

What I realized though is that this is my truth. It has resonated with me in a way I know to be true. I know when I am in a state of focused thinking, and I am receiving thoughts from Universal Wisdom, what I am receiving are not my own thoughts as I feel it, and the wisdom is too vast and meaningful to be something I could know on my own.

I even struggle at times to be able to find words to match the knowledge I am tapping into. In fact, I have to write down these thoughts when I am in this focused state as I would not remember all of them later. I also realize that as a teacher, those who resonate with this knowledge will find me, and they will know if they believe this knowledge to be true based upon what they feel when they are reading it.

This leads me now to what I wanted to know next as I explored Universal Wisdom. What is interesting is that I have so many questions to ask as I tap into Universal Wisdom that sometimes I am not certain I know where to begin. But for this time, during my focused thinking, I wanted to know about making my presence known in the field of teaching others about this knowledge and wisdom.

My questions included: If I am to become a teacher, which I am willing to become, how does a man or a woman make their presence known in the world? How do they shine a light, as just one person, in a world filled with millions of people? Will my path lead me or must I forge a new path and create this new journey now?

I will share with you what I have learned about another one of the Laws of the Universe, called the Law of Presence. This can help you find your voice, whether it is in your personal life or in your professional career. It may help you in your own journey of self-discovery and self-development.

A universal truth is this: Every man, woman, and child are present in life, sharing in and nurturing the essence of life which creates and sustains the endless energy source.

This presence creates a universal connection through which energy is sustained and balanced, and through which signals of life are emitted and transmitted to Collective Consciousness and higher order Universal Wisdom. Even when a person's physical form is shed, or the human form is released, the energetic form still remains, still connected, still flowing, still present, yet no longer physically seen.

When Someone Loses Their Physical Form

Many people believe that once the physical form has been shed, the connection is gone. For those who have a religious point of view, the person has been transported to a fictional heaven with pearly gates, or a fiery pit to pay for not following the right set of rules as dictated by a vengeful supreme being. Either way, the connection to this person, one who was loved, beloved, deeply cared for, and/or admired, is believed to be lost to those who remain here with a physical form.

One Law of Attraction teacher tells followers when someone leaves their physical form, that person's vibration changes - and someone who is in a physical form can only connect with that person now if they are in a happy state of mind. It is understandable to teach the idea of a positive focus. But connecting with a non-human entity, or a soul as some would call it, does not abide by rules. This is energy, life energy, which we are all connected to and part of at all times.

We all have unlimited access to this energy. The question is how willing we are to tune to and listen to the vibrations and frequencies of this energy. A person who loses their physical form is never lost, and they are never only found in happiness only. Yet, if you are focused on their passing event only, your sadness will distract your ability to listen and focus to their energy form now.

If someone you care about has been present in your life, their presence creates a permanent connection. It is often experienced in a more subconscious rather than conscious manner, as to how this person will now communicate, guide, or reach out to you. You will notice it more in subtle moments, rather than direct communication. And you do not need to worry about perfect conditions either, when you want to reach out and feel the essence of their energy. You only need to relax into it, trust you are able to access this type of energy, allow your fear to subside, and enjoy listening.

Career Questions and Presence

Your presence on Earth, in physical form, creates a permanent connection with those you care about, admire, and love. Your connection also extends into the world. You are connected to life, to mankind, and to the universe. Every physical human is a presence.

The question which a man or woman often has is related to their career, and how to advance and improve. The answer is not a matter of how to be present in a career, it is how to be heard. Someone can be present on a job, but not be heard. Being heard is not about being the loudest either, it is about being noticed, called upon, and relied upon.

To be present and heard means you have a voice in what you are doing. You have a unique point of view and you are living a fulfilled life. For a person who has not yet found this in their career, it means their presence is in a job, but they have no voice yet or a small voice in what they are doing. This person has not been heard.

Not every person needs to be heard to have a successful career. Some people only need to be present and complete the required tasks. Others will have a specific purpose to fulfill. The need to be heard can push a person to find their voice and clarify their mission or purpose statement. Each person needs to understand the purpose they have created for their career and then seek to shine a light on their presence. This is a time to draw upon the insight of Universal Wisdom, to see what happens next, and listen for inspiration.

Finding Your Way, Fulfilling Your Purpose

To fulfill a purpose, a person must find a way to make their presence known to a majority. That is an important step if the purpose felt is to rise above and chart a new career path or goal. When a person feels as if destiny is calling, that means their life's plan is unfolding and they are being guided towards it. Now this makes it sound as if someone is in control or a universal team is assembled and waiting to help, but that is not so. It means a person established the plan prior to arrival in physical form and put challenges as checkpoints which would help to prompt the right action along the way.

Often challenges, problems, adverse conditions, health situations, and anything unexpected that causes a person to look within, can propel a person to the point they do something which causes their physical presence to be known by many, their voice to be heard, and they are living what feels like a fulfilled life. Struggles, pain, upset, loss, and tragedy are all often pre-planned challenges to wake a person up and allow their voice to be heard through an innovative or new solution. Not all people need to be heard though in their career. Some people can complete their tasks and work with a task-related job. But when a person feels there is more to do in their career, that means their presence needs to be awakened and their voice heard.

This becomes a transformative time in a person's life, when a career is not catching up with the desires or interests of the man or woman. This is why one job alone may not fulfill the need or allow a person's presence to be known and voice to be heard. This is also why reaching a majority of people is key for someone who feels they have a special destiny to fulfill. Take a best-selling author, pop singer, television show personality, or famous chef. They all began as being present in the world. Yet they felt a special destiny or calling or purpose. They may have had one job or a series of jobs. But eventually their presence was made known by the majority in their field. They found ways to ensure their voice was heard, people listened and followed.

In contrast, some people have routine jobs with daily tasks that do not change, and they enjoy it. Their voice does not need to be heard at this time by a majority. They are part of the energy system which supports the economy and the nation, giving life through the work they produce, which is also serves a vital and important purpose. Even those who do not work serve their own pre-planned purpose. They have decided before coming into physical form what their purpose will be, and they have decided how their presence would be made known, whether in relationship or support of someone else. But everyone is connected to the energy of life and supports it in some manner. All of this is based upon the Law of Presence.

The Law of Presence

The Law of Presence states that all humans are present in this world with their physical form and connected through the source of life energy. This presence allows for connections with others, some of which will transcend time. The degree to which a person is present in this life is dependent upon the path a person is to follow, and what degree their voice needs to be heard. A person can be present for a short time or for the long term, heard by a few, or heard by thousands. Every person has a specific role or purpose they are fulfilling, and their energy helps to nurture and sustain life energy.

Presence can fluctuate. For example, a person can live quietly and on their own until one day they meet a person they will connect with and build or cultivate a long-term relationship. Now their presence has been transformed from low energy to higher energy. The same can be said for presence in any situation. A presence can be quiet or loud, the same as a person's voice, physical or metaphorically.

But to reach your dreams, new career heights and pinnacles, and to achieve the extraordinary, a person must become present to many, their voice clearly heard, and they must be able to nurture new connections. Those who reached this level of presence have their insight available in higher order Universal Wisdom, available to inspire and teach the artists, writers, creators, inventors, entrepreneurs, and anyone who is willing to listen, believe, accept, and evolve through their guidance and inspiration.

Law of Presence: Fulfilling Your Purpose Summary

<u>The Law of Presence states</u>: A person's presence in the physical world does not depend upon status, the path traveled, career, or any other factors established by man. A person is present at the moment of physical arrival from the source of life energy and lives according to the plan decided upon while in pure energetic form.

Every human being serves a greater purpose while present in this physical world. In addition to fulfilling a life plan, each person is also causing the source of life energy to expand. Each human being is still part energetic form, which means all new memories and knowledge and wisdom are stored in the Collective Consciousness. The positive energetic memories are stored in the positive energy spectrum and the negative energetic memories are stored in the negative energy spectrum. This causes the energy source of life to continue to expand and this nurtures all of life and all of the universe.

Each person has already decided what their presence in this physical world will be like, including the challenges and pleasures to be experienced. It will also include the length of time to be present in the physical world.

As a person goes through life in the physical world, there is often a belief that circumstances, events, people, and even decisions made are the determining factor for outcomes experienced, the quality of life, and how life is lived. Yet there are no random events, rather there is a planned presence. This is not to state life is fixed in place as every plan can vary and some plans may allow for options and flexibility, based upon the free will nature of man. Yet outcomes are known, agreements with others made in advance, and connections put into play as determined by plans.

This changes the nature of what is taught by religion, which involves instilling a belief in control by a higher power and supreme being. But those who see past this are able to take back control and gain the most clarity about their lives. This in turn allows them to live life to the fullest, fully aware, engaged in life, and awake in their presence.

The Law of the Duality of Energy: Experiencing Negative Emotions

When you have experienced the loss of someone close to you, or you have felt a time of sadness so deep and personal, and the only way you could describe it was to explain it as pain, you are likely experiencing grief. Almost everyone has experienced this type of grief in their life, whether they have lost a loved one, family member, close friend, or even a cherished pet. Any time we bond with another living being, and we lose this physical connection or relationship due to death, it can create a deep void.

I have experienced grief in my life. One was the significant loss of a parent, and the other was the passing of a beloved family pet, which may seem insignificant to some, yet this furry friend was a loving being who gave love unconditionally. One loss occurred as a result of tragedy, and circumstances I could not begin to imagine. The other was a decision my spouse and I had to make because of our pet's declining health, and a mutual agreement was reached with our veterinary physician.

What happens during a time of grief is a period when the world may seem out of focus, when emotions are felt deeply, and there may be a range of thoughts from sadness to loneliness, or from guilt to shame during this period, until a sense of becoming clear-minded can occur once again. It is not possible to predict how long a period of grieving will last as it is individual in nature, and the cause of the loss or event also determines how long the recovery will take. Those who remain focused on the past and refuse to look forward usually find it takes even longer to recover.

I am an educator and teacher, not a licensed psychologist or counselor, yet I have studied how adults learn, along with cognition, the development of belief systems, and basic psychology. What I have learned, through my studies and interactions with students, is how the nature of grief can change a person. It is almost as if a person is wearing a mask for a period of time, as they do not feel themselves or appear to others to be the same person. Anyone who is trying to help someone who is grieving may feel rejected or unable to reach through to them, and the reason why is simply that this is a deeply reflective state. It is also a personal time, which may be difficult to express.

As a teacher of Laws of the Universe, I have already come to understand there is energy associated with grief, as there is with all emotions. Within the source of life energy there are positive and negative energy spectrums. It seems as if grief would be associated with negative energy as there are no happy or joyous feelings associated with it. Yet I cannot imagine how grief is the same type of negative energy as anger and hate. Those are destructive and often violent forms of energy.

Then as I have been connected to Universal Wisdom and sought to learn more about this subject, I began to understand there are different types of negative energy. The forms of negative energy already mentioned, anger and hate, that energy is associated with intentional, negative energy streams. In contrast, grief is an unintentional, internalized negative energy, something which a person can experience growth from in time, use as a learning opportunity, and eventually transform from as healing and renewal take place.

I found this knowledge of different forms of negative energy streams to be enlightening, and I wanted to learn more since I too have experienced grief, and I wanted to help others. I will share with you more about what I have learned as I have connected to Collective Consciousness and Universal Wisdom, about different forms of negative and positive energy, and the Law of the Duality of Energy.

A universal truth is this: Human beings consist of energy, it is why each and every human is in existence, because of having energy. Energy serves as a power source, that which fuels and transforms the physical form. The source of that energy is the source of life energy, what some would call source, God, the Divine, or other names to infer a Supreme Being. But energy exists and always has existed. Energy is intelligent, it is not a random blob that is pulsating at will. This is why the cells within a human's body are able to carry a program and a code, and why a human body can go through a life cycle.

The Human Body

The human body has a brain, the center of the energy within a human's body, helping to direct and control many of the bodily functions. The brain operates on energy, without direct input from a human, as it relies upon its connection to the source of life and a connection to the Collective Consciousness. Within the brain of a human are energetic currents, flowing to and through, allowing a human to experience its environment as sensations, feelings, and emotions. All of these elements are energetic in nature.

Energy as a Stream

Just as energy itself is balanced by positive and negative energy, to keep it sustained, so too is every energy stream. Every energy stream, like an electrical current, is balanced with a positive and a negative current. The two spectrums must be present in order for energy to exist.

Now consider the emotional state of a human. There are positive and negative emotions available, and within every human. Every person is going to have both currents of emotions within them, as energy cannot exist without them. These emotions are energetic in nature and they are also experienced energetically. This means a person can never ascend to a state where negative emotions have been eradicated from their being. It can never happen.

The positive emotions could be experienced as joy, happiness, bliss, excitement, appreciation, gratitude, peace, contentment, and anything else related, which elicits feelings of intense well-being within a person. It is the best of all feelings. The negative emotions are those which elicit the worst feelings, such as hate, fear, dread, anger, rage, killing, punishment, and the list continues.

But not all emotions experienced by a human are clear cut as to being the best or the worst. The question about grief is a good example and the notation about grieving not equal to hate is correct. When a human is experiencing grief, it is a negative emotion, but from an internalized state rather than a position of provoked emotion and one directed towards someone else. This introduces the Law of the Duality of Energy.

The Law of the Duality of Energy

Energy is positive and negative. Yet it is further divided by another duality. This is where the law can provide clarification. The distinction has to do with the manner in which the emotion was brought about to begin with. An emotion of grief is generally brought about by loss. A person experiences the absence of someone or something and does not know how to adjust to this new reality. This is when the grieving starts. This is negative energy as it is generally not productive.

Now consider an emotion of hate. This is a very strong current, usually one which has been cultivated over time, and directed at someone, something, or a group of people. It is extremely negative and unproductive. It is also internalized but very self-damaging, and it only worsens the longer it goes on.

In contrast, grief tends to improve in time as coping mechanisms are found, whether by finding natural insight and wisdom, or relying on the strength of others. But this shows that even within positive and negative energy, there are dual natures as well. Within the positive energy spectrum there is the Positive Sustained Energy and the Positive Replaced Energy. Within the negative energy spectrum, there is the Negative Sustained Energy and the Negative Replaced Energy.

Sustained Energy: This is inclusive of practiced emotions. It involves practiced patterns of feeling happy, miserable, lonely, sad, hate, angry, the victim, or any recurring emotions. These emotions can change, but it does take time and concentrated focus.

Replaced Energy: These are the emotions which are experienced daily and are short-term in nature. For example, a person can feel happy on Monday, but on Tuesday they are feeling down. The person has experienced Replaced Energetic emotions. As another example, this week a person lost a friend and now they begin grieving for a few weeks.

This person is experiencing the start of Negative Replaced Energy, until the grieving period is passed. Replaced Energy emotions are not practiced long enough to be sustained into a chronic energetic state. These short-term emotions allow a person to learn and to grow, even if it only means learning to get out of a bad mood for a day.

If a person is not getting stuck in a particular energetic emotional cycle, they can be more aware of how they are feeling, provided their emotions are not going from high to low every day. The idea of being able to learn from grief comes not from the emotional energetic experience, but from the time when the person is finally able to listen for insight and wisdom during a time of loss.

Guidance During Grief

During grief, there is a lot of attention put onto the memories of who or what was lost, which creates a mental barrier. This does not cut the person off from their connection to the Collective Consciousness, but it can be distracting. A person can receive insight and clarity at any point, happy or sad, if they are willing to stop and listen.

Those with a religious upbringing may pray and seek guidance from a Supreme Being. When insight arrives, it appears their prayers were answered. What actually happened is the person quieted their thoughts long enough for wisdom to come in. Though waiting on a higher power to do something may cause even more disconnection when the answer needs to come from within, rather than from someone or something else.

Relief from Grieving

So, when grief has found a person, the first step towards improving a person's state of being is acknowledging that negative energy exists and resides in all of us. In other words, do not fear the feeling of grief. You can embrace the human, natural emotion of grief, as long as you understand there is wisdom available to you and inside of you.

Then the quickest way to move from a Negative Replaced emotion, to something positive or a feeling of a positive energetic emotion, is to reflect not on the loss itself of the person or whatever or whoever it was that is now gone, but the joy of the of the being that was in your life. This creates positive energy and positive emotions, which then creates or begins a process of internal change. Now you can start to think in a positive frame of reference, and then you can refocus your mind and thoughts towards a new reality. This will allow wisdom to flow to you and through you.

Your purpose in life is to live a fulfilled life and you do this by living and experiencing a wide range of energetic emotions, both positive and negative. To be human is to know how to feel both positive and negative emotions. To awaken and be enlightened is to transform negative energetic emotions to a positive state, rather than allow chronic patterns of negative energy to set in.

When you can experience emotions and transform them, you are then able to learn from what you feel. This is also how you can gain the most clarity and insight from the Collective Consciousness of mankind and Universal Wisdom, as you are now attuned and listening, ready for growth, healing, recovery, and receiving insight about the plan you have created for your life. Yes, you may grieve as it is natural, but in your grief you can find joy, and when you do you will be transformed.

The Law of the Duality of Energy: Experiencing Negative Emotions Summary

The Law of the Duality of Energy states: Energy is forever balanced with positive and negative spectrums, never considered right or wrong, balanced by the dynamics of contrasting memories, emotions, stories, intelligences, and other human perspectives. It is where positive and negative energy spectrums meet, a neutral zone, that the Collective Consciousness of mankind resides. This is the active presence within the universe which is the source of life energy. It contains the consciousnesses and life plans of all humans.

It is from this collective that energies decide to develop a plan and extend their energy into the physical world. But the extension does not separate from the collective, rather it remains energetically attached. This allows memories, stories, and other human perspectives to continually flow into the energy spectrums. When the physical form ends, the body returns to Earth and the energy simply exists again in a pure energetic state.

Summary of Energy: Energy is neither circular or any other shape. It is formless yet exists all around the universe. It is the air, the wind, the planets, and all of life. It is living, pulsating, breathing, and without end. The word "energy" itself is the only word within the English language which best can describe what this entity is.

What is challenging for humans is to think the source of life energy needs no control, especially by a supreme being. But energy is already alive and fully functioning, serving to power all of life. It can never cease to be as the positive and negative spectrums continue to exist and grow as human beings add to it every second of every day.

The Duality of Energy also means: A human being exists with both positive and negative energy streams, just as energy matter itself does. A human being needs both forms of energy to remain balanced and alive. It is not possible to exist with only one of these types of energy streams. Where a person can take note of the difference between positive and negative energy is through their mind and how they experience feelings. Those feelings allow a person to state they are in a positive or negative frame of mind, which means they are experiencing positive or negative emotions.

A challenge for many humans is believing they must be positively focused at all times, never allowed to feel negative emotions or experience negative circumstances. A positive focus and positive frame of reference does help create a happier and more productive day. But to fear negativity is to live a life of bondage.

The negative emotions, displayed through feelings of anger, being impatient, upset, or anything similar, are only a natural part of the energetic process of being human. It is a reminder that energy is balanced within, through positive and negative energetic streams. To remain negatively focused is to become destructive or internally distressed, but to acknowledge and address those feelings is to learn how to balance your energy.

Self-Reflection Worksheet:

What do I feel?

What do I question?

What do I want to explore?

What do I want to ask?

How have my beliefs changed?

How have my views changed?

CHAPTER 5.
THE IMPORTANCE OF YOUR MINDSET

When you awaken to the knowledge of the energy of life, and the Collective Consciousness of mankind, you begin to realize how you have immediate and unrestricted access to the wisdom and knowledge of all of mankind. But how is this possible? How can you have this access without asking for permission from someone?

It is possible because you are connected through the power of your mind. It is through your mind that you are connected to the source of all life itself, the energy which nurtures and sustains all life forms and all of the universe. Every human being has immediate access, yet few allow this access as most establish mental barriers that restrict the natural ability to attune to the Collective Consciousness. But once you awaken, or reach a point of enlightenment, you are set free and can benefit from Universal Wisdom.

Consider how the mind operates right now within you:

> Your mind is connected to the energy of life and is never cut off from it. You may establish mental filters which restrict or slow down the access you have to wisdom and guidance, but you can never lose your connection to the source of life. The energy of life is flowing to and through you, creating a subconscious energetic flow and balance within you.

> Your mind is also connected to the Collective Consciousness of mankind. As you are thinking, your thought forms are contributing to the Collective Consciousness and energy spectrums. The negative thoughts are drawn to the negative spectrum, and the positive thoughts are drawn to the positive spectrum, with both spectrums sustaining and nurturing

the energy of life. This connection to the Collective Consciousness also provides a pathway for you to gain access to Universal Wisdom, if you allow yourself to attune to the positive spectrum and listen for this insight.

At this very moment, your mind is acting as a generator for your physical form, while maintaining connections to the energy of life and the Collective Consciousness. It is directing the automatic functions of your body, without needing your direct or conscious input or control.

Your mind also has a conscious capacity, the aspect which is referred to as thinking, processing, analyzing, etc. This is the part of mind which is under your direct control, the function of the mind which you can attune through focus and concentrated effort or allow to become unfocused. While focused and attuned, this is the aspect of mind which receives Universal Wisdom and insight.

This demonstrates the amazing capacity of the human's mind. Yet what is even more spectacular is the ongoing activity of the mind at a subconscious level. While it may seem as if the primary function of the mind involves the thoughts a human is presently thinking, in reality that represents only one of several perpetual functions. Yet to a human, this is the primary function of the mind as it is a conscious process and a person cannot really ever be consciously aware of a subconscious process. But the outcomes of a subconscious process can be witnessed and it provides evidence to support its existence.

An important question then for a human is this: How does a person coordinate the conscious mind with the subconscious mind to live an empowered life and benefit from the Collective Consciousness of mankind, and access Universal Wisdom? You do this by attuning your conscious mind to the positive energy spectrum, which means you have set an intention to have a positive mindset each day, and follow the insight or guidance received. It also means you believe in your dreams, follow the images you have that are associated with your dreams, and look for indicators which will show you how the plan for your life is unfolding.

For me, I have learned to be open and listen to my inner voice and trust my internal guidance. Anyone can connect to the Collective Consciousness and higher order Universal Wisdom. It takes practice to focus and allow inspiration and wisdom to come to you. This is especially true for bigger or important subjects, as Universal Wisdom may not translate easily into the knowledge a human mind currently possesses. It also requires removing fear, especially removal of the fear that has been instilled by religious organizations that wants you to believe you cannot have direct access to this knowledge and wisdom on your own.

I have had a powerful connection my entire life, although I did not always understand or accept it. More importantly, it did not agree with my religious upbringing and it was a struggle at first to reconcile this conflict and then overcome it. It also took time to discover the source of peace and balance this connection could provide. Once I learned to accept and understand it as a natural human connection, I found tremendous inner peace and harmony. Now I quiet my thoughts and focus, even in a noisy place, although I prefer a peaceful environment with soft ambient music.

One of the teachers of Law of Attraction who has helped me in my journey, presents this wisdom through channeling. I see this as a form of theatrical presentation, as a means of providing higher order wisdom from someone or somewhere else. Consider this perspective: If you thought the wisdom being provided was just coming from that person, rather than a higher being or Collective Consciousness itself, would you be as likely to believe it? The presentation of wisdom through channeling is similar to formalized religion. It is dissemination of infinite knowledge from an authorized person, meant to create dependency on that person. If that person taught strategies to enable people to be independent, they would listen once or a few times, and not need to come back.

But what this teacher does is to access Universal Wisdom. It is accomplished through focused thought, which is something anyone can do. This is why I began to write and share my own journey of awakening. I am still discovering the purpose for my connection and how to live an empowered life.

I do know there are others like myself who want to learn more than Law of Attraction alone can answer, and I will continue to explore the many other Laws of the Universe. What I can tell you is that when I am connected to Universal Wisdom, I feel a sense of peace and well-being. If you can discover this for your life, it can help you sustain a positive mindset.

The topics presented in this chapter include: How to tap into and benefit from universal wisdom, how to find answers to important questions, how to find relief from feeling overwhelmed, understanding the higher purpose of gratitude, and how to keep a positive outlook about life.

How to Tap into and Benefit from Universal Wisdom

Would you like to know how you can make your life better, even if your life is calm or going smoothly now?

I believe at some level we would all like to know how we can improve upon our existence. I certainly would as I think about the age I am at in life and how much more I would like to accomplish. I have a career as an educator and teacher I would like to continue to nurture, and I have always found it has been natural for me to help others as I am one who can patiently guide the way through a learning process. I have a deep understanding about how adults learn, what motivates them, and how to nurture and encourage their progress.

In 2017 I have had an awakening, coming into a full realization of my connection to the source of life we are all connected to and it has helped me realize what I have felt inside all of my life. I now better understand that being a "sensitive" and "quiet" person really meant I was reflective in nature and I could easily listen, to myself and others. When I listen to others, it means I can sense what they are feeling, not just hear what they are saying, and I can even do this through electronic communication. This may sound odd but I have been teaching online for over 12 years and have learned to communicate in a virtual environment, which helped me take my ability to listen to an entirely new level.

Every time I have had a specific question, it has prompted me to listen for answers. This helped to strengthen my connection to the energy of life we are all connected to. Since I do not have a religious perspective, and rejected religious dogma long ago, it is easy for me to settle in, relax, and focus on just listening for an answer. Several years ago, when I first discovered Law of Attraction, I thought I was going to find something life-altering, which would cause my life to suddenly change. I filled in blank checks, created vision boards, and became determined I was going to live my life a certain way.

Did my life turn out the way Law of Attraction teachers said it would, after many years of following their practices to the letter? The answer is no, despite becoming very good at following their practices. Does this mean I failed in some manner? No. Does this mean that the Law of Attraction failed in some manner? No. What is the problem? There isn't a problem, except in the teaching of it. If you follow these teachers, you generally see the same group of people, asking the same questions.

The Law of Attraction teachers, especially one who is most prominent in teaching this subject, generally talks around complex subjects rather than provide direct answers. This was important for me to experience as it pushed me to keeping searching and asking questions. One of the first questions I wanted answered was about how to tap into Universal Wisdom.

A universal truth is this: The mind of a man or a woman is the living connection between his or her existence and the energy of life, which is connected to the Collective Consciousness of mankind and Universal Wisdom.

It is this connection which mankind, through organized religion, has named a soul - in an attempt to describe how human existence could be connected to non-human existence. But to call it a soul makes it sound as if it resides on its own and acts on its own, which is purely a work of fiction.

It is the mind of a human which transmits and receives signals at frequencies that are so high and subconscious, both at the same time, life flows to and from these signals. These signals come as thoughts, ideas, impulses, and inspiration. Whenever a man or woman seeks knowledge or wisdom, this is how it flows to him or her.

Seeking a Connection to Universal Wisdom

There are those who seek to know how this connection works, how to better access Universal Wisdom, and how it may be possible to benefit from it. Those are usually the teachers and the seekers of knowledge who live an enlightened state.

Being enlightened is not magical. It does not equate to wealth or power, or even perfect health. It does mean the seeker has established a peaceful existence with self, even if the body is imperfect. Mankind is challenge oriented and health challenges are not different, they are pre-planned and created to prompt a person to seek answers, as part of their journey to enlightenment.

A path to enlightenment is also a path to self-actualization, an awakening to one's self and one's truth. Some people, in fact many people, plan for their entire life to be a series of steps to enlightenment. Very few people want to arrive in a physical existence fully aware, all-knowing, and living their truth without any challenges. That would leave no lessons to be learned, no reason to call upon, access, and use knowledge from Universal Wisdom. A human's existence is usually meant to be imperfect, to be the contrast needed to sustain the world and balance the energy source.

The Quest for Knowledge: How it Begins

Some who seek knowledge and answers to life gradually come into their truth, realizing the fallacy of religion, and they begin to experience life in new ways. They seek other teachers to help understand what they are experiencing, hoping to find explanations for what they are feeling, and a desire to learn how to evolve. They begin to understand in time that they too are part of the source of life.

Accessing Universal Wisdom

Anyone can access Universal Wisdom, the highest form of life energy in Collective Consciousness. It is a matter of tuning in with intention and purpose. A teacher of Laws of the Universe is someone who can listen and is able to quickly set aside all other thoughts in their mind.

They can trust the thoughts or impulses being received as transmissions from Universal Wisdom are not their own, but in fact are coming from another source. This takes practice, it requires suspending self-doubt, and it necessitates having a neutral mindset, one that does not judge any subject but allows information or thought forms to come through.

A teacher will usually write or speak as focused thoughts come through. Writing is the best medium as the writer will usually not remember everything once coming out of a state of focused thought. Some people use the word meditation but it is really focused thinking. Starting with a question is helpful as it provides a launching point for focus, as Universal Wisdom is so vast and deep - without a starting point it would be challenging to receive a strong set of ideas or block of wisdom.

Those who seek knowledge are the ones who find it in Universal Wisdom. Accessing Universal Wisdom through a human's mind is usually a gradual process as it takes practice to tune in, to focus, and then receive such powerful knowledge from the source of life energy. Sometimes a human's limited vocabulary slows down the connection during focused thinking.

No Limitations to Universal Wisdom

Those who seek Universal Wisdom for selfish reasons are not restricted from doing so. There is no person or supreme being dictating terms of use. There is endless energy sustaining life, and a Collective Consciousness base of knowledge which is Universal Wisdom. Those who think they can find magic somehow, through "Source Energy" or "Infinite Intelligence" by gaining lottery numbers, or acquiring a new house or car, or something else, usually are disappointed as they are not looking for wisdom - they are seeking instantaneous relief, solutions, and results. That is not a question for Universal Wisdom and even if the knowledge came to a person for how to acquire one of these items, they likely would not be listening for wisdom, only quick answers and solutions.

A True Path to Fulfillment: Accessing Universal Wisdom

A person who is on a quest to find fulfillment in their life, who wants to evolve, understand, grow, live, create, travel, write, paint, create, and so on - they will be the ones who easily access Universal Wisdom and gain knowledge and wisdom. The wisdom received may be small insights, or life altering moments of awakening.

A person can receive Universal Wisdom even when they do not understand fully what it is they are receiving. For example, a deeply religious person calls it God and prays that they receive insights and believe when it happens that it was from God. They then live a happy life. The wisdom they received came in through a disguise. However, this person will not live a truly authentic life by receiving wisdom in this manner, but they still have access to Universal Wisdom just like every other human.

Anyone reading this now is likely to already be on a path of enlightenment or awakening to their truth. You are already beginning to understand your connection to the source of life, and your journey has led you here. You have direct access and you can continue to nurture this connection as part of your journey.

A teacher is also important as you can learn from someone who is highly practiced in focused thinking and likely to be further along in their journey. A teacher can help you learn about the valuable Laws of the Universe as well, which will guide you in your journey, until one day you have become the teacher yourself.

How Do You Find Answers to Important Questions?

Do you have questions right now, about your life or your career, which seem to be so important, so big, or so personal that you do not know how you will ever find answers? I have and this has prompted me to consider how people search for answers, when they have questions which touch their hearts and are deeply connected to their being and very existence. Those people who hold a religious perspective about life will pray and seek answers from someone who they believe has the ultimate authority to make decisions and determine if they are worthy of receiving the answers sought.

But as a teacher of Laws of the Universe, I have learned this is not how life exists. I know we are responsible for our own existence, and have already made a plan for our lives, one which exists at a subconscious level and unfolds as we progress through life. I know there isn't a supreme being who decides if we are worthy or not worthy, ready to condemn us for our mistakes, as our imperfections and mistakes are part of what creates life and leads to greater understanding and wisdom.

I also have learned that contrary to many Law of Attraction teachers, the universe is not waiting to assist us either, as if there might be a team waiting to provide us with the resources needed to create our dreams. I know we have already made our plans and we discover them when we dream, along with the times when we create, write, paint, draw, or seek other forms of inspiration. What may seem like assistance from a supreme being, or a universal team, or even appear as a miracle, is all part of a plan which was put into place before we arrived - and we made arrangements for those components to line up, just as they have done in proper time.

But now at this point in my life's journey, I find myself asking questions about evolving and becoming. I want to know how to become the vision I have held in my mind for some time. I know how to focus my thinking and connect to Universal Wisdom, and this was my point of reference as I sought to gain clarity and wisdom, to help myself and others who may also have these questions. I will share with you the knowledge I have gained from Universal Wisdom about evolving and becoming.

A universal truth is this: Within man's mind is the access to all wisdom, all knowledge that ever was and ever is. When anyone speaks of the mind as being limitless, it is due to no one being able to ever specify the exact limits of what a mind can store or transmit as a signal or receive as a signal. The mind is complex as the universe itself, as it is made of energy, it is source energy, the source of life, the connection between the physical form and the energetic form, which remains even after the physical form is shed.

Understanding the Complex Mind

The mind is called a filing cabinet as it seems to store or retain vast amounts of information, yet this is somewhat misleading. The mind of a human is energy and is connected to universal Collective Consciousness, where all knowledge is retained. As a person "learns" or gains new knowledge, this knowledge becomes not just available to that person, it is now knowledge stored in the vast and unending Collective Consciousness.

When a person needs to recall this knowledge, signals are activated, and cognitive scientists assume the information comes from within the human's mind. Yet the mind is energy, it is not a static form, or a box with papers in it. It is living and transmitting. The signals acquire the knowledge and the storage location is a combination of human and Collective Consciousness. When a person seems to forget something, and tries hard to remember, but doesn't until later, that is the mind changing signals in a search for the knowledge in Collective Consciousness, like a query in a database search.

Searching for Answers

Understanding the complex nature of the mind is an important starting point in a person's awakening and learning about Laws of the Universe. Many people spend their lives searching for answers, about their relationships, jobs, health, future, finances, and so on. People seek out religion as they are taught to follow the rules and if they do so, they will be properly rewarded. They also know they can ask for special favors by praying.

Others seek teachers and hope those teachers will guide them. Some will help, others will teach some helpful ideas but not go far enough to empower their students. And many people seek books, magazines, and online resources to tell them how they can find answers to make their lives better. But relying on others, or reading printed words alone, does not lead to finding the true knowledge.

Finding the True Knowledge

The true knowledge a man or a woman needs, especially when they have very big or personal questions, is accessed through the signals transmitted and received in their mind. All is accessed within the mind. When a man or woman has what seems like questions that are too big to answer, it means they are on a path of awakening. To awaken means you are becoming aware of your presence. As stated by Law of Presence, you must be present in the world and your voice must be heard. It also means you are living your purpose and what feels like a calling.

When your questions feel too big about your life, it means your presence is awakening in the world. There is opportunity yet for you to find how your voice can and will be heard, perhaps in a metaphorical or a symbolical manner. No matter how it is happening, you are in the process of becoming.

What it Means to Have a Dream

The feeling of having big questions also means there is an awareness on a subconscious level, a signal being received by your mind, of a plan you had already prepared - and it is ready to unfold, or perhaps elements of it are ready to begin unfolding. This is what is meant by having a dream. A dream is not really what humans describe. You have already planned your life and made arrangements for events to take place. What dreaming actually means is that you are receiving visual reminders of your plan - and it is meant to encourage you to take action at certain times, also as planned. It is possible your plan was to allow for options, or to give you images, knowing you would never follow through with it. But when it is strong as a visual image, and stays with you, it is real.

Big Questions and Finding Answers

The feeling of big questions is a matter of trying to articulate what the plan for your life is, when that really is not what you need to be concerned about. When you need to take action, as related to your life's plan, you will know what to do. Your mind has access to all of the details of the life plan you have already created. Whenever circumstances seem bleak, trying to understand the bigger picture may become even more important. But that will only disrupt your signals and cause you to become focused on negativity.

The best approach is to savor the images you have of your dreams. Then all of those feelings related to a bigger plan will guide, inspire, and help you answer the challenging questions you have now. All of the questions you have can be answered as all humans retain access to Collective Consciousness and Universal Wisdom. The answers arrive not in your time, but according to your planned time.

What You Need to Know About All Questions

This applies to the big questions a person has about their lives, something personal in nature, something which is directly related to their future and existence. It is possible this will involve a financial matter such as overwhelming debt or a matter of well-being. Those questions are complex and do not have immediate answers. Those questions also cause people to find teachers, churches, and self-help resources in a search for answers.

There isn't a quick fix or immediate answer to most questions of this nature as it is usually tied to a person's life plan and their blueprint charted a specific course. There may be visual images or dreams to serve as positive reminders and help keep the proper signals transmitting in the mind. But the mind is ever connected to the energy of Collective Consciousness and the answers will be transmitted as planned.

This is in contrast to routine questions or daily questions a person has and can be answered through access to Collective Consciousness. It usually happens as "aha" moments, inspiration, or "I have an idea" types of moments. But that is how vast and expansive the mind is. This also explains where those seemingly random ideas come from, the Universal Wisdom from all of mankind, through the living energy of the mind.

The mind will never be fully explained, just as the universe is too vast to be fully understood. It exists, it thrives, it nurtures life, and all questions, both small and large, do have answers. This is similar to the design of life, which is balanced and carefully planned, just as the source of life itself, or the energy which sustains mankind.

The answers you seek are all within your mind, along with your life's plan. Your life is not randomly ordered or out of control. Be inspired by what you believe you imagine and follow the plan, where ever it takes you. This is how you thrive and this is how your big questions are answered.

Understand the Energy of Change

Do you ever wonder why change is so challenging for a person to undertake? Consider trying on a new style of clothing, perhaps a color you have never worn before. How uncomfortable does it make you feel? Or how do you respond to someone's suggestion you should change the style and color of your hair?

All of these thoughts are personal in nature and create feelings of uncertainty. But those emotional reactions are not limited to changes in a person's appearance. It can occur any time we are taken out of our normal routine. I'm certain you can think of a time when you went into a new environment, whether it was a new store or even a new city, and you felt disoriented.

Any time when we are removed from familiar surroundings and forced to change our perspective, it may be a time of great discomfort. How long it lasts depends upon how adaptable a person is and whether or not they are able to quickly reorient themselves to a new setting or mindset.

I have seen this happen as an educator, especially while working in the field of distance learning. When students attend a traditional classroom, there is a sense of normalcy and what can be expected. But with a technologically-enabled environment, the classroom can feel quite disorienting at first. This forces students to change how they communicate and how they learn. Now learning will involve more than using a search engine for answers or information. It also means learning to communicate in a socially respectable manner, rather posting online messages in an emotionally reactive mood.

These are changes, which like any change that causes a shift in thinking, which can be challenging to adjust to and take time to process. I understand we as humans can adapt to our environment, yet I wanted to learn more from an energetic perspective and this is what I focused on while connected to Collective Consciousness and higher order Universal Wisdom. I will share with you what I have learned about the energy of change.

A universal truth is this: Energy is ever flowing, moving, alive, and pulsating through all of life, and all of the Universe. This energetic flow creates an ongoing cycle of growth, productivity, renewal, regeneration, restoration, and return to form. This energy is in constant motion, yet is able to solidify at a cellular level, atomic level, microbiotic and particulate level, to create life.

This solidification process appears unmovable to humans, and yet as energy, everything still returns to form. A piece of wood can rot and return to the Earth. A brick can lose its form and break down into dust. The human form decays or declines, or can be forced to end its course, and becomes separated from its energy source. Nothing remains or lasts without end except energy, the energy source of life. And for energy to be in motion, for this cycle of life to occur and be ongoing, there must be changes happening at all times. Nothing and no part of life can ever remain unchanged.

The Mind's Coping Mechanism

Humans, society, culture, all of life evolves, grows, and expands through a process of growth and change. Due to this constant cycle of change, the human mind has established stabilizers to help humans feel a sense of security in their daily experience. If humans all felt the energetic cycle going on, and flowing through them, there would be tremendous discomfort experienced by many. The human mind has developed a coping mechanism called habits.

Habits of the mind are the routines or patterns of thought a person establishes to put order to their day. These are the mental shortcuts used for completion of tasks, from something as simple as remembering how to use a kitchen appliance, to directions needed for driving to a job. With habits firmly established, a person can feel a sense of stability - even as brief as it may be, while everything else in life is changing around them.

Changing a Long-Term Habit

Changing a long-term habit is challenging, not just because it is a mental or cognitive process, but due to its energetic nature. When a person decides to willingly change some aspect of their life, or some habit of their mind, there is positive energy associated with it. Yet the idea also puts the person in a cycle of change, which is energetically different.

Feeling good is only a starting point and sustaining this positive feeling does help with the management of change. But the energy of change is busy, dynamic, powerful, sometimes forceful, and very active. A person needs more than a good idea to want to change. They need true intent, a positive feeling which is sustained, and active involvement in an ongoing change process.

Motivational Changes

The motivational industry, along with many other self-help industries and spiritual teachers, utilize the idea of change and self-improvement to help draw followers in. Yet when the results promised are not received or experienced, there is a common belief that the followers had a lack of follow-through, or simply lacked any ongoing interest.

As an example, if someone attends a motivational seminar and learns a new habit of thinking which is guaranteed to make them wealthy, they usually leave with an intent and a positive feeling. Soon afterwards, the energy of change becomes more active and now those who attended the seminar begin to realize something must happen.

Yet over time, another realization occurs, when people begin to acknowledge there is more involved in the process than what was learned in the seminar. In other words, the thought of change alone is not enough by itself to create a change.

Many people who attend motivational seminars feel the initial positive intent, but cannot match the energy of change required later, and this is why long-term success is rare for these types of seminars. Many report these seminars fail due to participants forgetting information within a certain number of days or lacking sustained motivation. While those factors may contribute to not receiving the outcome expected, the ultimate cause can be found at an energetic level.

Involuntary Change

Now consider change which is forced upon a person, someone who does not seek out an opportunity to change. This could be a person who has experienced loss, whether personal or professional. Now this person is forced into the energy of change. The disorienting feeling is a result of the active nature of this type of energy.

Change is a state of energy which requires action. A person who experiences it must, at the very least, acknowledge it. It can disrupt habits of thought, which pull a person out of their routine, and this may create negative feelings or emotional reactions. Unexpected, traumatic, and forced change are the most difficult to adapt to.

Learning to Adapt

A person who wants to learn how to adapt to change can best do so from an energetic perspective. In other words, work inwards first, before addressing external conditions. To begin, address what is being felt and experienced on an emotional level. This is how to find the energy change within.

This is how a disruption can be pinpointed, if negative feelings are experienced. If this is a positive experience, looking within will be easier, as the energy of change can be felt and managed much quicker. What is meant by this is trying to feel the new sensation of the event which occurred, how you responded to what has happened, and how you internalized it.

Once you have done the internal work, you can then begin to shift your mindset and perspective as needed. You can ask yourself: How do I need to adapt? How can I adjust? Has my view of life changed and if so, what will I do to accept it now? How can I embrace this change and grow?

Change is neither positive or negative, good or bad, from an energetic perspective. It is a catalyst for growth, development, learning, and renewal. As you learn to adapt to change from an energetic level first, you will find it easier to adapt to it, whether you need to change habits, emotions, attitudes, or beliefs.

After you complete the internal processing, any external actions taken will be done as a result of your acceptance, not your resistance. As you learn to accept change from this perspective, you then discover how you are growing and evolving as a human being, one who is still an energetic being.

How to Find Relief from Feeling Overwhelmed

Do you want for your life to expand and become more than what it is today? Do you wish to do more in your career, but feel blocked, stalled, and unable to progress? Do you have wishes, desires, hopes, and dreams which never seem to come true? Whenever you find yourself with questions like these, and you feel as if your life or your career is stuck, or life is coming at you faster than you can handle, it can all begin to feel overwhelming.

As I have been connecting to Collective Consciousness, and listening to higher order Universal Wisdom, I can feel the vast amount of wisdom which is available for every man, woman, and child to access at any given time. It awakens within me the dreams I hold, which I know now are visual reminders of a plan I have already created for my life.

Yet as I am able to visualize those images, and I can experience the vast expanse of the universe while I am in a state of focused thinking, I can also feel the weight and pull of reality all around me. For example, I have friends and colleagues who want more from their lives, they seek to be free of debt, find new jobs, become fulfilled in what they do in their career, or create a life in which they do something meaningful. It is challenging to stay in a focused state of happiness when there is so much unhappiness that seems to be all around us in the world, or when the responsibilities of our lives start to build. Whenever reality becomes too much for a person, this is when it becomes possible to feel overwhelmed. What I wanted to explore further, as a point of gaining clarity while connected to Universal Wisdom, is how to find relief from feeling overwhelmed.

Something occurred to me as I examined my practice as a teacher of Laws of the Universe. It may appear I am telling people there isn't a God. First, I would like to assure you I do not wish to change what you believe as we are all on different points in our spiritual awakening. As a teacher of Laws of the Universe I have seen behind the façade created by the religious institutions and know the truth about the idea of a God and a devil, and how it was put into place as a form of societal control.

In addition, to become an awakened teacher I have had to learn what the true source of life is and who is really in control of this universe. There is a source of life, there is an energy to life, there is a universe sustained by the source of life. All of mankind is connected to, nurtured by, and sustains the source of life. You can choose to call this source of life whatever you believe. My purpose as a teacher of Laws of the Universe is to show you that you do not need to wait for someone to help you with your life as you are in direct control of your life. More importantly, you do not need to live your life in fear of being punished that you did not live it correctly. You are the source of your own life and you are the creator of your life.

Now I would like to share with you what I have learned from Universal Wisdom, about finding relief from the feeling of being overwhelmed.

A universal truth is this: Every man, woman, and child have a mind which is actively transmitting and receiving signals and impulses, no matter what condition the human physical form may be in. The mind transmits and receives multiple signals at any given time, with this energy flowing to and from the source of life, the energy that sustains mankind and the universe, and is nurtured in turn by mankind's mind and energy.

Mankind has described the mind in many negative ways; a scattered mind, a monkey mind, an unfocused mind, and a forgetful mind. In truth the mind is receiving and sending many signals concurrently. The signals are an energy and through these signals, knowledge, wisdom, and memories are transmitted through vibrations to Collective Consciousness. The wisdom gained by mankind is stored in higher order Collective Consciousness called Universal Wisdom.

Understanding the Signals of the Mind

Understanding these signals is essential to knowing the function of the mind, which can lead to learning about the order of the universe. The mind is in a constant state of transmission and in constant flow with Collective Consciousness. This means there is an ongoing stream of knowledge flowing to and from it, along with an ongoing stream from what is referred to as memories.

A memory is not just filed away in a drawer somewhere. It is fluid, living, dynamic, and easily accessible. Those humans who planned a life with a health challenge or injury, which limits their brain function and seems to turn off some memories, was done as planned to create a new or different life, one which is free of those past details or events.

Events are happening all around a human, at any given time. Noises, the environment, sights, sounds, smells, all of this is creating signals and vibrations. While many believe the mind can only process so much information, which is true, the signals of the mind are in fact sensing and picking up on all of it. There is a lot of stimuli coming in, and a lot which can also over-stimulate a person's mind.

The Balance of Positive and Negative Energy

The source of life is the energy which sustains the universe and mankind. Energy must be balanced, which means there is negative on one end of the spectrum, and positive on the other end of the spectrum. This is how energy sustains Collective Consciousness. There is the negative spectrum, which consists of negative emotions, feelings, experiences, and events. There is also a positive spectrum and this contains the positive emotions, feelings, experiences, and special occasions. This is how

Collective Consciousness stays balanced, yet there is no physical divide between the positive and negative spectrums other than the energy field, and it is easily accessible by all of mankind.

What it Means to Become Overwhelmed

Becoming overwhelmed is a condition where the mind is developing too many strong signals that are negative energy based. It may be outside input, such as news heard on the television, or events that occurred during a person's day. When a person starts receiving negative input, and cannot filter or process it well, it becomes a strong reactive negative signal in the person's mind. Then other negative signals within the mind are activated, such as past negative events. This is what teachers of Law of Attraction mean when they state: a like thought attracts another. But it is not that simple.

There is actually a process going on and a reason why a person who has a negative thought will begin to have more negative thoughts. It is a system of signals in the mind being activated. On a typical day, the mind can and will balance a person's thoughts. Some negative input will be received, but it will be processed in and out, without activating too strong of a signal or for too long of a time period. But those who reach a point where they feel overwhelmed, to the point of feeling depression, grief, giving up, or despair, have negative signals which have been chronically activated. There are positive energy signals still present; however, those signals have been minimized. It is a matter of how a person trains their mind to focus.

Finding Relief from Being Overwhelmed

Once a person has reached a point where they feel overwhelmed, how can they find relief?

Understanding the mind's system of signals helps a person know what to do but switching from negative to positive signals is not going to be an immediate occurrence, especially if this has become a practiced habit. What the person needs to do is begin to find moments of relief. This means finding, creating, or nurturing moments of happiness, enjoyment, fun, creativity, or anything else which can light up, from an energetic perspective, a positive signal. This should be something which feels good, maybe even selfish, whatever will bring about pure joy, even for a few moments to begin with.

Involvement in anything fun, uplifting, or creative is certain to help. Even the physical gratification of sexual relations with another human, or one's self, can elicit positive feelings. This is a universe based upon energy and when a human's physical form experiences joy, happiness, pleasure, or bliss, it radiates through their mind, and transmits through their mind as an energetic signal and transmission to Collective Consciousness.

The more moments a person can purposely set out to create, the stronger the positive signals become, and the less the feeling of being overwhelmed is experienced. Soon the person's disposition is transformed. This is all within every person's control. Every person's mind is theirs to develop, nurture, and attune.

Feeling overwhelmed does not need to last and the sooner you can nurture positive signals, the sooner you can go back to seeing the visual images of your dreams, which will allow your life's plan to continue to unfold without any interruptions. When you are feeling overwhelmed, those signals can interrupt the imagery of your dreams, which remind you of the plan that is unfolding in your life, along with reminders of the steps you are to take and this can slow your plan down. The sooner you can get back to nurturing positive signals, the better you will feel, especially as you focus back on the dreams of your future and what you have planned for your life.

What Is the Higher Purpose of Gratitude?

Is it important you feel grateful for your life and everything you have in your life? Do you need to show gratitude, or love and appreciation, for life and those whom you love on a daily basis?

A popular topic within the field of self-development, especially spiritual self-development and Law of Attraction, is gratitude. This is a referred to as a positive state of emotion, which has been attributed with numerous benefits, from maintaining a well-balanced disposition to living a healthier and happier life in general. Those who practice gratitude do so by being thankful for what they have and more importantly, demonstrating this appreciation by showing compassion and kindness towards others. It is believed when a person feels appreciative, glad, and happy, their overall well-being is likely to improve - mentally, emotionally, and physically.

As an educator and teacher, I can understand the purpose gratitude serves, especially the role of appreciation. If I can see the best in my students when I am working with them, rather than focus on their deficits, it allows me to build from their strengths and this instills a sense of hope within them. I believe every student has an ability to learn, no matter what their background may be or what they believe about themselves when they begin a class or make an attempt to learn. This is a form of gratitude as I am thankful for the ability of each person to learn and never stop learning.

As I am becoming more connected with Collective Consciousness and Universal Wisdom, I am interested in the purpose of gratitude from a higher order perspective. I can imagine it is on the positive spectrum of energy as it is connected with an emotion of love, happiness, and peace. This is also where Universal Wisdom resides and is both sustained and maintained, within the positive spectrum of energy.

What I wanted to know is whether or not this particular human emotion or feeling has greater meaning since it so highly valued from an emotional, physical, and mental perspective. Why does feeling grateful mean so much to the human experience? Does it also influence the source of life energy which sustains mankind as well?

I have always felt a natural connection to the emotion of appreciation. When I was working on my doctoral studies I needed to develop a subject for my dissertation, and while looking for research topics I attended a seminar about appreciative inquiry, which was actually outside of my field of specialization. I was enrolled in an Adult Education program and this seminar was in the business field, yet the topic sounded very intriguing.

Once I learned about appreciative inquiry, it became a subject I have continued to study and apply to this day. My dissertation research study took appreciative inquiry and adapted it for distance learning and online teaching. This means I understand and apply the act of appreciation within my own life. Now I wanted to learn if appreciation and being grateful extends beyond our human form.

Accessing Universal Wisdom

Mankind is living energy, a stream of energy flowing to and through a physical form. The mind is the conduit of this energy, and a gateway between the physical form and the energetic or unseen existence, which remains in existence even after the physical form is gone. The lessons learned in life by humans, or the knowledge and wisdom, becomes part of Collective Consciousness called higher order Universal Wisdom. This Universal Wisdom has no gatekeeper, no set of vibrational doors, no supreme being guarding it - and it is available to all humans and can be accessed by anyone. Yet this Universal Wisdom is rarely accessed fully.

Those Receiving Degrees of Access: Mankind has created a system of religious institutions to enact order and societal control, to dictate the morals of each particular society. Each institution defines what the unseen means and creates spiritual imagery and beings to represent something which cannot be easily explained. Those who follow a particular religion may find access to a limited amount of Universal Wisdom, through creativity, writing or other means that allow themselves to remove the mental constraints they have been taught. But when they believe someone controls the universe and their lives, their ability to tune to a higher order frequency is greatly diminished.

Many people leave religious institutions when their being tells them through internal discomfort that what they are taught is wrong or does not align with what they know to be the actual truth about the existence of mankind. Some will quit and never look further for answers, and others will continue to evolve and begin to transform.

Those with Natural Access: There are those who are not encumbered by religious perspectives who can naturally attune to Universal Wisdom. Some people who do this live their lives in peace and bliss without ever stopping to realize what it is they are attuned to, they just know that through quiet meditation and trusting their inner voice and instinct, they can live their life to their fullest and be happy.

Those with Access Who Share It Partially: There are those who are well aware of the connection they have to Universal Wisdom but they only share it with a small planned program or in a carefully planned manner. They may have learned one particular lesson from Universal Wisdom and chose to focus only on it. These are usually teachers who either want to develop dependency among their followers because they are afraid of losing or not retaining their followers, or they may only understand some of what they have tapped into themselves. They may not always present the direct wisdom gained, just their version or some version of what they have learned.

Those with Access Who Share in Full: This writer has had a natural ability to attune to Universal Wisdom but it took many years to really understand what this meant. It also meant shedding religious ideologies and dogma engrained from childhood. This journey also included shedding the teachings of many of the Law of Attraction teachers, who either use what appears to be a mystical and inaccessible channeling process, or a process that may or may not work in the manner described.

What this writer has come to understand can be summed up as follows:

This is not a "gift" as this ability to attune does not require being anointed by a supreme being or special access granted by a divine authority. It takes time, practice, and trust in yourself as you have to believe you can have access to this wisdom without fear of being punished by someone. You also need confidence to know these thoughts and ideas are not your own, and you are not making words up as you are thinking or writing them.

This is not what some would call automatic writing. The writing which occurs while this writer is in a state of concentrated or focused thinking is simply a matter of taking notes while in a vast library, searching for information about a variety of topics. This writer does not disappear or go somewhere else. He is still conscious and present, he can have others present in the room, though his ability to concentrate would not be as focused if others were making a lot of noise. Having a question is always a good starting point to begin a query. Once the information is accessed, it can be described as accessing pages of information and this is where the written notes are coming from as quickly as can be written on paper. This writer has nurtured and developed a strong signal or connection with Universal Wisdom. There is no question now where this wisdom is coming from and this writer is taking notes as fast as he can while he is tapped into it. This writer wants to share this knowledge with others just as he experiences it. There is no need for the theatrics of channeling as his life plan was to tap into and share this wisdom.

This now ties into the primary question held about gratitude.

A universal truth is this: Mankind has discovered they can be happier when they are thankful, but not just thinking about how much they appreciate their lives, actually showing how grateful they are in some manner.

The reason why gratitude matters from a physical perspective is that it creates a very strong positive energetic signal that reacts down to a cellular level. A person who has been labeled with clinical depression will rarely spend their days talking about how grateful they are for what they have in their life now. Yet if they could embrace that mindset, a change would begin.

This ties in with the word appreciation, as it carries the same energetic vibration. The act of appreciating one's self, as well as others, causes quite a shift at a cellular level, even if practiced on just a few but genuine occasions. The question now this writer has is whether these forms of expression, gratitude and appreciation, matter at a higher level or universal level. The answer is that everything occurring within a human is influencing all of mankind as mankind is linked by energy.

The Energy Spectrums

Energy is balanced with a negative spectrum, center, and a positive spectrum.

Negative Spectrum: The negative spectrum is where all of the pain and past hurtful events of mankind have gone. While the negative spectrum does not nurture the energy or source of life, it must be there to balance it. This is how energy exists, with a positive and a negative dual existence.

The Center of the Spectrums: The center is where the Collective Consciousness resides. It is a neutral place of all memories of mankind, stored for reference and access. This includes all of the life plans each human has created and energetically stored for themselves. It is a knowledge base and it is within this knowledge base where that this writer begins his query to seek knowledge of a topic or subject.

Positive Spectrum: The positive spectrum is where all of the positive emotions reside, including love, gratitude, and appreciation. Within the positive spectrum is where higher order Universal Wisdom is accessed, the wisdom and knowledge of all mankind. This spectrum is nurturing the source of life, and it is from this spectrum that physical forms emerge. This is also why people who claim to have a near death experience state they have seen a bright light. It is the process of shedding the physical form and a person's energy emerging back fully into the positive spectrum of the source of life energy.

The answer to the question sought about the connection between gratitude and its effect on the source of life energy is this: Any positive emotion or feeling serves a human well from a physical to an energetic perspective, and it radiates all the way through to the source of life energy itself. The practice of gratitude and appreciation can start with one simple thought, or act of self-appreciation, to begin a process of energetic self-renewal. The more this is practiced, the more this is likely to become a habit. This is how humans experience long-term health benefits and increased happiness, as a shift occurs not just in the mind, but in the cells of a human's body.

How Do You Keep a Positive Outlook About Life?

Have you ever considered how you can stay positive about your life when it seems you can never get a break? How can you keep a positive outlook about life when you face daily challenges, such as overwhelming responsibilities, financial debt which continues to grow beyond your ability to repay, and/or health concerns which may further limit your ability to perform your very best? Is it possible to sustain happiness and find balance in your life, even during those times when circumstances are less than perfect?

Whenever you read self-help resources, you will find a constant theme related to the importance of being positive and happy. There is a belief you can think your way to happiness, and this is even the basis of Law of Attraction as the underlying premise is about like matter attracting like matter. Yet I have worked with Law of Attraction long enough to know there are many people who can think about being happy, and never seem to attract enough similar thoughts to remain in a happy state of mind for long.

This is not to state there isn't value in the work of positivity or positive psychology. I have been teaching the importance of a positive mindset as an educator and now a teacher of Laws of the Universe, which means I understand how valuable this frame of mind can be for someone who is able to achieve it. When a person is able to feel positive, it means they are attuned to the best emotions they can experience and this is related to their belief system. If they are attuned to positive emotions, they may believe in themselves, and this is when someone is more likely to succeed when there are new goals, dreams, or aspirations they want to achieve.

However, I know the reality of maintaining this state of mind. A person can feel empowered when conditions in their life are good and it appears as if things are going their way for them. What happens for many people is that they look around and see their reality, and this is what makes self-empowerment challenging to sustain. Negative events or occurrences are hard to tune out or ignore, and simply stating an affirmation isn't going to change someone's mindset quickly. This is why people state reality is real. You cannot avoid it and when there are emotions attached to it, it can affect your state of mind and how you feel about yourself.

What I have learned as a teacher of Laws of the Universe is that there are energy spectrums, both positive and negative. It is the balance of the two spectrums which sustains this universe and creates the source of life that we are part of as human beings. We, as human beings, all have access to the Collective Consciousness, which is a repository of positive and negative memories. There is also a higher order Universal Wisdom, which is the product of the positive spectrum of energy. It is the essence of the wisdom of all of mankind, and anyone who is focused and attuned to the positive spectrum can access this Universal Wisdom.

This wisdom is what I am able to access while I am in a concentrated, focused, and thinking state. Yet this wisdom does not give privileges. Even though I am a teacher of these laws, I do not live a life of ease. I maintain normal responsibilities and I do not have access to special secrets of the world. In other words, I do not possess special powers as a teacher or command authority as if I were a religious leader either. I am a teacher through my experience and background.

What I wanted to know while accessing Universal Wisdom is how a person can attune to the positive spectrum and sustain it. More importantly, must a person maintain a positive attitude at all times, in order to live a life of balance? Will attunement to a positive spectrum at all times assure a person lives a life of happiness?

I'll share with you what I have learned about maintaining a positive outlook about life.

A universal truth is this: Every human is a product of energy, which sustains all of the universe and life. To understand the nature of man is to know that man is part of the source of life, and through the actions taken while in physical form, man creates energy, and this sustains, nurtures, and balances the energy of life.

Those who seek to understand the nature of man must be willing to open up to and experience universal truths. One truth is that man's mind can never comprehend and/or accept how energy came into being. The nature of energy is infinite and man's mind is finite, even with a connection to the Collective Consciousness. There are not enough cells within the human mind to hold the knowledge of the nature of the source of energy.

What man did when language was formed, was to create a myth about the origins of the existence of humans. Since man cannot understand the origin of the source of the energy of life, it had to be (according to a human's rational mind) someone or something else who created the universe, including all living things. Every culture created a supreme being or beings and assigned it power. There were rituals assigned, along with ceremonies and rites, creating a formalized system with specialized roles.

Cultures eventually organized groups around belief systems about these supreme beings, each group deciding to be the one holding authority to dictate access and interpret the knowledge received from this supreme source. Then man saw an opportunity for power and control. Yet real teachers, such as Jesus himself, was but a man who could access Universal Wisdom - and he was someone who did not approve of organized religion. His words have long since been altered in the highly edited document still used by religious institutions to this day.

Understanding the Nature of Energy: Positive and Negative

Man exists in physical form, still connected to the energy source of life. This energy source of life is sustained by the positive and negative spectrums. Within the positive spectrum is the very best of mankind, from the great inventions, to the happy memories, to the very feelings of joy experienced.

Books and articles about personal self-development often focus on well-being and the importance of a harmonious state of mind. These sources may emphasize mindfulness, gratitude, appreciation, joy, bliss, or other words and phrases associated with living a positive life. The purpose is to be or become a happy person, and by doing so, your life is supposed to become better, more balanced, and you may even be physically healthier.

Within the negative spectrum are all of the "bad" memories of mankind. This includes pain, hurt, regret, loss, suffering, or anything else man has endured, experienced, or suffered. To try to understand the nature of man, one must truly understand the negative spectrum. Yet most people fear this subject or avoid the painful topics. Religions of all kind have established this spectrum as evil, and some religions have assigned a fallen angel or a red devil who resides in a fiery pit to it.

This includes the punishment for failing to live according to the standards established by a particular religious faith, or by a supreme being's rules. It also represents what would be called sin by these religious groups. From a societal viewpoint, this is the reason why most laws have been made as the negative spectrum also represents what would be the crimes, the violent acts, or even disobeying the laws of society. It is the essence of doing everything that is considered to be "wrong" according to society.

Also, within the negative spectrum are the emotions of sadness, despair, loneliness, and so on. When a person attunes to those frequencies, it means they do not connect with the guidance which is available to assist them, or they have intentionally chosen to avoid facing the reality of life around them - and they have found no other coping tools or strategies. When a person can no longer instinctually accept what religions teach and have no other teachers yet available to guide them, they may attune to the negative spectrum and an emotion which is seen as less than desirable.

This is also true for someone who no longer wants to be controlled by society and then focuses on the negative spectrum, attuning to what might be viewed as breaking the laws in some manner. If a law is broken, it may be done as an act of defiance to speak out against a system of controls.

Both religions and society seek to control the actions and thoughts of mankind. It is all directed at keeping mankind in a positive spectrum or doing the "right" thing. But many people do not act in this manner and this leads to campaigns, a war against various criminal activities, holy wars, world wars, and so on.

Seeking world peace really means seeking dominance by one particular society as no two cultures or religions will ever agree on how to define right and wrong, or who has authority from the supreme being. More importantly, world peace cannot occur as the nature of man cannot change.

Sustaining a Positive Mindset

This leads to the question about sustaining a positive mindset or learning to attune your mind to that frequency at all times. Every man, woman, and child are here in physical form with a plan for their life. It is challenging for many people to accept, that they are the ones who are responsible for their lives, but there was a plan created and it was foreseen in great detail.

Now in order for the energy source of life to be sustained, there must be positive and negative energy. This knowledge is important. It means the world cannot and will not live in blissful peace, with everyone smiling, getting along, and never fighting among each other. There will always be conflict. This is also important as it means mankind will always experience events, circumstances, memories, and more, which are negative in nature. No one will live and not experience something from the negative spectrum.

Just as the energy source of life needs negative energy, so too does the existence of every human. Does that mean someone will chose to live a life existing fully within the negative spectrum, such as the life of a criminal, to fulfill their life's plan? To answer that question would unravel so many teachings of religion it would be called heresy. Just know the balance of life requires positive and negative energy.

Can you stay in a blissfully positive frame of mind at all times? It is the pursuit of this question which has caused more unhappiness than happiness. Even if a person lived on a mountain top and had unlimited wealth, challenges would arise at some point in time.

Attunement Towards the Positive Spectrum

Instead of focusing on how to live in a state of bliss, develop an attunement towards the positive spectrum. Have an unwavering belief in yourself. Believe in what you are capable of, even when challenged. When negative events or circumstances occur, remember this is part of balancing energy. Use your positive beliefs, memories, love, and any other similar feelings to guide you. Then you will experience insight from Universal Wisdom, especially when reality seems so real to you.

The negative spectrum is very real and it is also very active from an energetic level, just as active as positive energy. Live your life by following your dreams and finding ways to allow Universal Wisdom to come through, whether in writing, meditating, reflecting, contemplating, or being involved in something creative. The goal is not about the pursuit of happiness. The ultimate goal is about living your planned purpose and attuning to the Collective Consciousness source of life for guidance.

This is how you develop a positive outlook. Will you stay attuned to the positive spectrum even when challenged? As you become more practiced in attuning your focus, circumstances and events will not deter you for long. But do not be concerned if you find yourself focused on the negative spectrum at any time as it is a natural part of the process of balancing energy. It will happen not by doing what is expected or what is right, but what fulfills your plan and brings out the best in you every day.

CHAPTER 6.
READ AND BELIEVE

Now that you know about Collective Consciousness, and the Laws of the Universe, what do you choose to Read and Believe? If what you have read stirs something within you, and you can believe in the power of your ability to attune to the wisdom and knowledge of mankind on your own, it then becomes possible to begin a personal and spiritual awakening. You are not dependent upon a religious affiliation, a teacher, or a supreme being to access and possess this knowledge as it is already available to you.

What you need to do is to accept you have the ability to control your own mind and learn to attune your thoughts in a focused and controlled manner to the positive energy spectrum. From there you can access the wisdom of mankind and receive knowledge and insight. You may receive direct thought forms once you are focused in meditation and reflection, or you may receive it through indirect forms such as inspiration, creativity, or other "aha" moments that allow you to tap into the infinite knowledge.

As a teacher of Laws of the Universe, I do not expect you to have an established set of beliefs or take on my set of beliefs either. I do not want to change who you are or what you believe as this is personal to you and who you are. I will share with you the knowledge I have gained while connected to Universal Wisdom and present it as I have received it. There isn't a right way of accepting this knowledge or believing in it, as all of us have access to this same insight. More importantly, we are all on different points in our journey of enlightenment and awakening, which means you may need something different, or be asking questions other than what I may have at this moment. My only wish is to share this insight with you and help inspire you in some manner.

The first topic addressed in this final chapter includes one of the most requested topics when people seek out answers to their lives and it involves finding abundance. The second topic has to do with being able to amend your life's plan once you are here on Earth as a human being. I hope that you gain insight as you read what I have learned while I was connected to Universal Wisdom.

How Do You Learn Self-Worth?

Can you state right now, and without any conditions or uncertainty, you are worthy to receive whatever you may hope for or dream about? Do you believe you deserve to acquire everything you want, as to the goals and dreams you have established for your life and your career? If something good were to happen right now in your life, or in your career, could you really and truly be happy for yourself, and willingly accept it?

Most people would probably answer yes to those questions, as who would state no when asked if they are deserving of the best in life? But the reality is much different, when you consider the mindset, attitude, and disposition most people have about themselves, along with the natural reaction they experience when they set goals, dreams, or a plan for changes in their lives. This also occurs when good things begin to happen and there is a natural sense of self-sabotage or a negative reactive current which begins to set in.

I believe at some level we all struggle, or least have struggled at some point in our lives, with accepting our natural ability to receive the good in life. There is a mantra about having to work hard in order to get what you want, and anyone who just inherits well-being was born with a "silver spoon in their mouth", which of course is a very negative connotation. This is just as negative as the belief that "money is the root of all evil". So many people want to achieve more during their lifetime, yet there is so much negativity surrounding the issue of actually accomplishing greater things or acquiring more in life.

In contrast, another area of self-development is over-emphasizing abundance, to the point it has taken one Law of the Universe and turned it into a magical, get rich formula. I am referring to the Law of Attraction, which is but one of many Laws of the Universe, and never meant to be the sole guide for anyone's life. It is a law about the state of a person's mind and is not the answer to every question someone may have about their life, relationship, career, or anything else for that matter. Yet there are countless books and teachers who have built entire teaching philosophies around it, and when it doesn't work for many people, this only reinforces the idea of a lack of self-worth.

This is also what happens when many people finally achieve the outcomes they hoped for, such as a new job, new relationship, new career, promotion, improved health, or anything else which had seemed to be something that had only been a dream. The patterns of reactive dislike and disbelief may set in, along with questions related to worthiness. For example, a person may question whether or not they have worked hard enough to deserve a new job, or they may ask if they deserve a new relationship. This may be followed by a critical self-analysis, and list of all of the negative qualities which seem to prove this new outcome or result or change was not deserved.

I have also struggled with self-worth. My reactive pattern, which demonstrated my lack of feeling a sense of internal worthiness, occurred whenever I would dream of becoming or doing or achieving something else. I would all of a sudden get upset about something completely different or unrelated to whatever it was I was dreaming or thinking about. What I have learned is that the outward signs of being upset were an indicator of the internal turmoil within me. I could see the dream, yet I felt the reality and it was all too real for me, which created internal conflict. How could I dream when I had obligations and other responsibilities which might seem to hold me back?

What this means is that I was not able to accept I could have a dream and move past my current reality, which also was an indicator I did not believe in my own self-worth. Once again, these were reactive patterns born from a life of struggle, and always trying to do what was considered to be responsible, rather than live empowered to follow a dream. This doesn't mean it was the wrong way to live, just one that was less fulfilled.

Perhaps this meant it took me longer in life to become a teacher as a result of it, yet I believe now all of these lessons were part of what I had to learn to now be a teacher. Now I can understand what it means to feel doubt and the reactive, engrained mental patterns. This is something I have learned and can help teach others now, about self-worth and self-love. This is also the subject I wanted to learn more about as I was connected to the Collective Consciousness of mankind and Universal Wisdom. I'll share with you what I learned about the energy of self-worth.

A universal truth is this: Every human being has a set of beliefs that are developed as a product of time and experience, yet the most influential formation time occurs early on in life. It is during the formative years when others are able to assert their influence on an impressionable mind, and this influence can last far into adulthood - even if the person creating or exerting the influence is no longer around or cared about.

Understanding the Nature of Beliefs

While beliefs can be changed, a person tends to form them early in life and then seek confirmation of those beliefs through life events. There are milestones in a person's life which can create new beliefs and are usually the result of aging, such as gaining experience and wisdom, and/or seeking out new knowledge and being intentional in a desire to learn and change. The beliefs which are hardest to change are those which are personal in nature, those deeply connected to a person's emotions and state of mind. In contrast, beliefs about the world, religion, politics, or other matters can eventually change through the acquisition of knowledge, wisdom, enlightenment, and through discourse.

But beliefs which are deeply personal and emotional are not so easily changed. Those beliefs typically involve how a person believes they look, how they believe they are fitting in with the world and their environment, how they are measuring up with others, how they feel about themselves, and how they view their overall worth. These beliefs are deeply held and engrained at an emotional, vibrational, and energetic level, held in a chronic pattern and sustained. These are long-term energetic emotional reactions and responses which become so deeply held, a person soon forgets they exist as they simply react in the same manner time after time.

For example, if a person has grown up believing they do not fit into society, this becomes a permanent, negative energy cycle which is so practiced they soon forget it is a belief. This person simply operates in life knowing they do not fit in, and any time they are put into a situation which may require them to try and fit in, they automatically respond in fear or reject the very idea of trying. If this mindset has been practiced long enough, it becomes a way of life until challenged. But to challenge a belief like this would require something to happen which would force a person to finally reflect and uncover why they respond to situations in the manner they do now.

Understanding a Lack of Self-Worth

One negative belief, which practiced long enough becomes a negative sustained emotion, is a lack of self-worth. This is one of the most self-defeating, negative emotions and self-beliefs a person can hold, simply because it creates negative automatic responses.

There are many reasons why a lack of self-worth can begin at an early stage in a person's life. The easiest answer is to blame one or both parents, and yet this overlooks the knowledge available about each person already having chosen their own life. The struggles which are part of life are similar to the steps necessary to create a diamond. The more abrasive the process, the better the outcome may be in the long-term. This does depend upon the purpose a person chooses for injecting challenges into their lives.

But problems and issues occurring early in life can weaken the natural built-in sense of worthiness available to every human being. This is exacerbated by religious teachings and conditions established by society. Feeling naturally worthy does not come easy for many people, not until they begin a journey of personal and spiritual transformation.

Understanding the Emotion of Worthiness

The emotion of worthiness is really about love. To feel a lack of self-worth is to feel a lack of self-love.

There are clues about how a person feels right now, regarding their belief about being naturally worthy. For example, a compliment, gift, prize, new dream coming true, or anything similar coming to fruition. How does the person respond?

If there is true happiness felt or experienced, the person believes they are worthy and deserving of what they are about to receive. In contrast, if there are questions, hesitation, concern, or any type of resistance which manifests itself externally through frustration, anger, depression, or any negative feelings - this person may not believe in their natural worthiness and the signs point towards internal turmoil. This also means they have not fully learned the art of self-love.

To love yourself wholly is to know you are here right now because you planned it, and you worked out the details ahead of time. While you may have experienced challenges early on in life, and do so even now, it never diminishes your worthiness to receive the best or whatever you dream of or hope for or desire.

Understand How to Love Yourself

To love yourself means you change the practiced emotion of disbelief into one of belief, so you can experience a better life for yourself, one without self-doubt.

The self-worth you hold is a product of the self-love you cultivate, and it radiates from within. You never need worry about asking for too much from life, as you are always worthy to have dreams - and through those dreams you will discover your life's plan and purpose. To embrace self-love is to finally accept life as it occurs each day, good or otherwise, with a practiced positive emotion of self-love, not a negative emotion of self-doubt.

If you have struggled with questions of doubt, and you are not certain if you have ever truly loved yourself, now is the time to develop a new belief system, to create a new life. You do not need a list of affirmations, or training for a new, positive mindset. Just a simple reminder to help you get started: "I planned my life."

This knowledge will begin to open many emotional doors for you, including love for yourself. The next reminder is this: "I have access to the Collective Consciousness of mankind at all times."

Now you are affirming your belief of self-love and self-worth. It is not tied to anyone and requires no one else to be involved. You are also not asking anyone to gain access for you, and you are not asking approval from anyone. This is for you and you alone.

The last reminder is this: "The wisdom and insight I need for my life is available to me and it can be found through my own mind."

With these reminders, you can now establish a practiced, positive emotion towards your life of self-worth and self-love. Now you are no longer needing to question whether or not you deserve something special in your life as you are living your life and connected to the source of life, the energy of life itself.

The more you nurture your self-love, the stronger your positive self-beliefs will grow. In time, you will learn to never doubt yourself or your worth again. Then you will be living your life to its fullest.

How Do You Find Abundance?

Do you ever want more from your life? Do you ever want to be abundant in some particular manner? If so, in which aspects of your life do you seek abundance? For example, do you hope to become abundantly wealthy, financially independent, or does abundance mean something completely different for you? Or perhaps you relate abundance to your health or well-being?

When I think about abundance, it can have a variety of meanings. Yet overall, I find abundance usually relates to the idea of having an improved life, whether it is an abundance of money, new career options, better relationships, improved health, or simply an ability to have freedom whenever it is needed. It is also related to questions people ask when they are looking for answers about their lives, especially when they cannot find answers through traditional religious teachings. There is often a lot of guilt associated with the subject of money, for those people who have a strong religious upbringing, as they have been taught about money being the root of all evil. For them, the thought of financial abundance or acquiring money easily, may seem wrong.

For this time of focused listening, I used questions about abundance. These were not questions about my life, but about abundance in general. For example, if someone wanted to increase their financial abundance, could they do so now or should they rely upon the plan they have already created for their life? In other words, can someone decide they want to get more out of life for any reason, and at any given time, and expect it can be attained? If so, how can they make this happen on their own and without the need for divine intervention? I will share with you what I have learned about abundance.

A universal truth is this: Look at the universe around mankind, it is alive and abundant in every way possible. To mankind, based upon limited vision, and even limited equipment to extend its sight, the universe seems endless. Mankind cannot seem to comprehend the abundance that fills the universe, even though some describe it as being void of life. The universe knows no end, it is sustained by the source of life, the energy unseen by mankind, which is nurtured by and gives life to mankind. It is sustained through Collective Consciousness and higher order Universal Wisdom.

This energy is alive and abundant, it pulsates with life, including the emotions and all memories of mankind. Through this energy source new physical forms are decided upon and come through, and then once present, the energy sustains its life until that physical form is shed. The energy of life is the most abundant example of a living entity mankind could ever begin to understand. There is no limitation as to how much this source of life energy can store and sustain.

Now look at Planet Earth: The areas untouched by mankind are some of the most abundant on the planet, usually consisting of wildlife and forestation. There is no restriction to its natural growth, without mankind's involvement. Much like the source of life, the energy which sustains mankind, there is no one who is controlling it. This is a form of energy with a physical form on Earth, similar to a human being. What you see in the waters and forests on Earth is a result of energy, with a physical form attached. Go to the oceans and forests, there you feel the most powerful energy on planet Earth.

Now look at the areas of physical Earth which are inhabited by mankind. There is not a natural flow of abundance. Resources are restricted and controlled. Some people experience great abundance, while others never seem to gain or acquire any measure of economic, financial, or other forms of well-being. Mankind also teaches that forms of abundance, such as the pursuit of money, are wrong or evil.

Abundance and Religion

The subject of money is typically what mankind relates abundance to and from a religious perspective, mankind is taught they must live a certain way, not commit egregious errors as defined by their particular faith and appease a vengeful and mighty supreme being who is in control of all of mankind, and all of the resources of the planet. This is living by fear, society controlled so that those with religious or political power can deem worthiness of a person and how much abundance they should be allocated. This is the ultimate universal smoke and mirrors trick, telling mankind that a supreme being controls them and they must obey this supreme being, when it is the religious institutions who made up the supreme beings for their particular faiths, and added the rules and guidelines.

It is only mankind which restricts any level of well-being here on Earth. The source of life, the energy which sustains all of mankind, does not dictate levels of well-being to each person. But because a person decides to come forward with a physical form into this physical world, they are aware it is a world of restrictions, rules, and not balanced for all to have resources equally. Many people will then develop a life plan which fits into this structure, to experience different levels of well-being, to be abundant right away, or perhaps struggle for most of their lives and receive it later.

Facing Reality

What all of this means is this: Humans can look upwards, see the universe, and know it is limitless. Humans can look at unspoiled areas on Earth and experience a vast sense of peace and well-being, the source of life itself. But then in the real world, the day-to-day life, the congested cities, the news, bills to be paid, the cost of housing and basic necessities; it is possible to see shortage. Humans see scarcity of resources. Humans see some people who are doing exceedingly well while others struggle in seemingly abject poverty. A person is given a value by being told that a certain dollar amount will be paid for a salary. Everything a person sees on a daily basis must be weighed and evaluated based upon what resources are available and accessible to that particular person.

There are people who then want more, they seek to have more, hope for more, demand more, and may even pray fervently to receive help for more. What does a person do at this point? A person often turns to those who dictate how resources are allocated. A person seeks out religious institutions, institutions which are often very wealthy, and is told to pray to a divine being. This is a limiting view. Who is this supreme being a person is praying to? Someone sitting on a throne who is easily angered?

How can you look to the universe, see the vast planets, know there are endless resources, then turn and plead your case to a being who may or may not be willing to grant your desires? Why would you want to believe life was ever really made that way?

What if there is no one controlling the universe? There isn't as the source of life is nurtured and sustained by the energy of mankind's memories and consciousness. Only a small percentage of the population awakens to this knowledge or planned to awaken as part of their life's plan.

When Man Decides to Take Action

When man rejects the idea resources should be controlled, one possible change occurs. A person may become an activist and work for humanistic causes. This is a type of awakening designed to help reallocate resources to those who are in need, or lack the basics needed to survive in the world created by mankind. There are many who plan for this as part of their life's journey.

When Man Truly Awakens

Another awakening is of the most immense, energetic type of all, when a person can see the universe not from the outside, but from within their mind. A true awakening occurs when the self-imposed limitations of abundance taught by man, and instilled within man's mind, are lifted. This is when a person's mind is open to "see" the universe. A person can then dream, and through those dreams, understand their life's plan.

Through the power of the mind, a person now knows there is no one controlling their lives or determining their worthiness to receive the well-being they seek. They see past the façade of a supreme being who is dictating terms or conditions. When a person can accept that truth, without fear of repercussion, they are the ones who awaken. They are also the ones who become the teachers and help others who are awakening.

The mind has direct access at all times to Collective Consciousness. You know how the words written here connect with you based upon what you experience in your mind, and by how you feel. If you can let go of fear and restrictions, you can feel an entirely new expansion of your mind. You can now awaken and experience life in an entirely new way. You can gain greater clarity and insight from higher order Universal Wisdom. You do not need to live in fear of being in shortage any longer.

How to Become More Abundant

So then, man wants to know about being more abundant. When people ask a question related to this subject it is usually about money and a shortage of some kind. The question about money needs to be changed from: "How do I become more abundant in this particular area of my life?" to "How do I discover and live the plan for my life?"

It is your life's plan which matters most. You are where you are at now not because of mistakes, or by accident, but because you are living according to a plan you already created. If you want to increase your well-being, allow yourself to awaken. Allow your mind to focus on the energy of the universe. Use your dreams as your guide. There are no rules or limitations. Allow your mind to open to life and the power of the universe. Follow your dreams and your plan will unfold. Abundance is available for everyone.

Can Someone Amend Their Life's Plan?

Do you accept you are in control of your life? Can you accept the possibility you have developed a plan for your life, even before you arrived here in physical form? Are you willing to reject the idea a supreme being or higher universal power is responsible for what is happening in your life now?

I have been studying the Laws of the Universe and the more I learn from Universal Wisdom, the more my mind has become open to truths about our lives. For example, I now know there isn't a supreme being who is in control of the universe. There also isn't a higher power who determines who has access to the energy or source of life. This has taught me every man, woman, and child has come forward in a physical form with a plan which he or she already developed and planned for in detail.

This was important for me to learn as a teacher of Laws of the Universe, as I have found I need to be open to receiving knowledge while learning the truths I have access to, as I receive answers to questions I have about life and our existence. Learning truths about the essence of our being and the source of life has been a transformational experience as I have come to know life from a completely new perspective. For example, now when I hear people state they are waiting on answers from a higher being, I want to say something to help this person learn a new truth.

I should make it clear I believe there is a higher power, which is the source of life. It is the very energy or source of life which connects all of mankind - those who are in pure energetic form, and those who are in both energetic and physical form. Yet I know this higher power does not dictate the terms of our life and does not control the source of life.

When people think of a higher power, they immediately have an image of a supreme being or authority figure who is judging them and their ability to receive some eternal rewards. What I understand the higher power to be is the power of the universe, the energy which sustains, nurtures, and maintains all of the planets, life, and mankind. All living and non-living matter nurtures this energy, and through new physical forms it continues to evolve and grow. All of mankind is connected to and has access to this energy state of being. There are no limits and no restrictions for access.

I have begun to write about what I have learned during this time of my awakening and personal transformation, as I want to share this with other people. I know Law of Attraction is but one of many Laws of the Universe, and the many questions people have about their lives may be answered by knowing these other laws. Reading about the Laws of the Universe can help to create a spark from within, as a person learns about their connection to the true source of life, and this can be transformative.

I recently shared my journey and what I've learned with my closest friend. I wanted to have the experience of helping someone else who has been studying Law of Attraction and not finding it to be transformational, no matter how many years she has tried to apply it or how many attempts she has made to follow the teachings of one of the prominent Law of Attraction teachers. When I asked my friend if she could accept the idea she created a plan for her life, and no one else did it for her, she replied and asked: Why would I create a life which was challenging at the beginning, and then challenging now during the later years?

We talked about the benefit and potential purpose of facing challenges in our lives, to us as individuals, along with all of mankind through the wisdom gained and stored in Universal Wisdom. She realized if she is indeed the one who created her life plan, and no one else is in charge, she would have to change many aspects of her thought processes. For a long time, it has seemed to her as if a higher power has been guiding her life and dictating how her life should be. She stated something which left a lasting impression: I wish we could go back to a time when we first met as friends, to a time when life was easier and there wasn't as much of a struggle.

This led me to my question for Universal Wisdom: Can someone amend their life's plan, once they arrive in physical form here on Earth? In other words, even though we have a life plan already established, do we provide ourselves with an ability to change it as we learn and gain wisdom through our life's experiences? I will share with you what I've learned about amending a life's plan.

A universal truth is this: Every decision a person makes has a ripple effect as it changes the course of their life, culminating in the path they have charted. Decisions are a form of energy as they carry a vibration, a conscious and unconscious thought process with each one of them made.

The seemingly conscious part of a decision is made as follows: I believe I have a certain number of options or choices before me and therefore I will make a decision based upon methods I have learned. I have learned to weigh the pros and cons, advantages and disadvantages, among other such strategies which allow me to rationalize the process.

The part of the decision-making process that is subconscious, or seeming unconscious to a person, occurs as follows: I make a decision based upon how I feel, or as some have called it, a gut instinct. Some believe those who make a decision this way may be prone to mistakes when they rely upon the heart rather than the mind, not realizing the unseen they are calling upon is the heart, which may be a source of greater wisdom than the rational thinking mind.

The Emotional or Feeling Part of the Mind

The emotional or the feeling part of the mind is the connection to Collective Consciousness, which is less restricted, less edited, and less subjected to personal biases than the rational thinking mind. This may go against conventional thinking, which proves the point. When a person has unrestricted access to Collective Consciousness and Universal Wisdom, they feel the positive energy of this flow. It is a nurturing and life-giving emotion, experienced as vibrations or signals coming to and from the mind.

The Rational or Thinking Mind

The rational or thinking mind is part of the process of being in a physical form and having a human brain. Now every person has this living organism which is capable of generating its own thoughts and ideas. It too is automatically attuned to the frequency of Collective Consciousness, yet it is a tuner and every person can adjust its signals. This is what is known as free will. This rational mind then is faced with daily decisions to make and while a person could learn to attune to Collective Consciousness alone for guidance, most people have learned to rationalize or think through these decisions.

The decisions being referred to are the types related to a person's life and well-being, versus decisions about matters such as choosing technical specifications for a piece of equipment in a person's job. Yet even someone who is highly tuned to Universal Wisdom and used to connecting to this wisdom could learn to rely upon it for every aspect of their life, from how to live, to how to work, to how to run a major organization. But very few masters could ever live and achieve this level of attunement and trust in themselves and what they were attuning to. The knowledge and wisdom are there to guide them, yet the rational mind struggles to allow control for matters involving something which is decided upon by the use of feelings rather than evidence.

The rational mind can be trained to accept Universal Wisdom as evidence rather than emotion alone, yet this takes time and practice. This is something the writer of this book has learned, to attune the rational or conscious mind to a frequency which receives Universal Wisdom clearly and as a trusted source of guidance. By doing so, this allows the many Laws of the Universe to occur in natural order. For example, the Law of Intention allows the intended life plan and events to unfold in the exact and proper timing. Another example is the Law of Presence, which these writings are helping this writer to experience now.

Understanding the State of Energy

Now with an understanding of the rational and emotional mind, the question being sought can be addressed, and it is about being able to amend a person's life plan. Consider first the state of energy. It is not a static substance, which means you cannot put it in a bottle or package it in a container. It is pure motion, always moving, flowing, evolving, and able to sustain itself. The source of life is energy, and it is nurtured by all of mankind. The new physical forms create new memories and generate new wisdom, which nurtures and helps to expand this energy of life.

All of this is important as the thoughts flowing to and from the energy of life are a form of energy as well. Thoughts are signals or vibrational impulses which carry and transmit information to and from the Collective Consciousness. This now leads to decisions, which are a thought form or series of thoughts. Every day a person has to make quite a number of decisions and every one of those are thought based. Just as thoughts are a form of energy, so too are decisions. All is energy.

Following a Plan, Determining Whose Plan

As a person is living their daily life, something else is occurring, they are following a plan. No life is randomly designed. This statement alone can be challenging for some people to accept. The next question involves whose plan is it. This is where religion comes into play and the teachings of a supreme being. There are other teachers who talk of source energy and infinite intelligence, almost alluding to someone or something else being in control. Most people have been taught, accept, and believe they are following a plan someone else created. They believe they were "put" here on Earth and they have to find their purpose for their lives, based upon what this supreme being or other worldly beings have decided for them.

To think outside of that is to reject religion and even the teachings of many spiritual or Law of Attraction teachers. Yet many people have done this and it is referred to as an awakening. It happens gradually as people reject the control held by religious leaders over the minds of their loyal followers through the use of texts which threaten punishment and eternal damnation for not following their rules.

Those who begin to question what they were taught do so because of what they feel, that somehow it just isn't reality. Once you can accept a new way of thinking, you can be enlightened. Then you can begin to realize that the source of life is what you are part of and the supreme being is you. This also opens your eyes to the knowledge that you did not just arrive here on Earth as a brand new physical form, without a past and without a past connection to the source of life. Even religions state you were born with a soul, which is actually stating you were born as an extension of the energy of life.

You were part of the energy of mankind, you decided to come forward in physical form, and you developed a plan to do so. When you came forward, you still are connected to the energy of life. How much you remember from your energy source depends upon your plan. This writer planned to have a strong signal to lead him to this point in time, to become a teacher of the Laws of the Universe.

Making the Right or Wrong Decisions

Once in a physical form, a person then is making choices about their life. It may seem as if their life is in flux, or that it can change from day to day. This is why a question would arise about being able to amend a plan. Yet all of this was thought out and anticipated in advance while you had the full advantage of Universal Wisdom, which is the wisdom of all of mankind. This means there are no right decisions or no wrong decisions being made, no matter how good or bad they may feel to you at the time. What you can do is to change your response to the outcomes. When you are faced with choices and you make a decision, which turns out feeling very good, state: This went just as I planned. When a choice leads to a decision and the outcome feels the exact opposite, state: This went just as I had planned.

Living Your Life's Plan to Its Fullest

You already created your life's plan and you are following it. When you seek your purpose, look for guidance from Collective Consciousness and Universal Wisdom to help understand your life's plan. How do you accomplish this task if you have never done this before? You learn to quiet your mind through reflection, concentration, or meditation, and try to listen for "aha" moments, your gut instinct, and positive emotions that seemingly come from the heart. It involves inspiration that comes during quiet moments and times of creativity. You want to live in accordance with your plan, to find and know peace in your life.

Interfering with Your Life's Plan

It is possible that you can decide to cut yourself off from being attuned to Universal Wisdom and Collective Consciousness, which you can never completely do in full because you are connected to the energy of life. However, you can choose a life of self-induced sadness and depression or become attuned to the negative spectrum of energy. You can choose to not listen to wisdom or understand your life's plan, which means you may interfere with the unfolding of your life's plan, or elements of the plan, or certain actions which need to occur as part of your plan. This again is referred to as humans having free will.

But this too may be part of your overall plan, or it may delay the well-being available to you by having access to the wisdom of all of mankind. There are still no right or wrong decisions to be made in your life as you are always on the path which is part of your life's plan. Even if you make a decision about something and you are certain years later you would have never done that by looking at the events again through a rational mind, you should know it is still part of your plan.

Should you decide to slow down or interfere with your life's plan, your life's plan never goes away. You are always living your plan, whether or not you consciously are aware of it. The awakening of a person to understanding how they created their plan also does not change or amend it, but it brings a sense of renewal and peace. It may accelerate their plan by opening new doors, increasing their well-being, but most of all, it returns empowerment which is often taken away through societal and religious controls. When a person awakens, becomes empowered, and realizes they are in control, they become more willing to take action to make changes in their life and this moves their plan, or necessary elements of the plan, forward.

Never worry about the plan for your life, just focus on finding attunement to the greater Collective Consciousness of mankind and Universal Wisdom, to gain clarity, peace, and understanding for your life's purpose.

What are Random Events?

We go about our lives every day, often with a plan in mind, but usually controlled or guided by the responsibilities we hold. Most of us hope to make the best of a day, or at least we try to get by, if we are working in a job or career we can only tolerate and it seems as if there is no certainty about the future getting better any time soon. There may be times when we feel stuck, afraid, uncertain, or in need of help, and all of a sudden someone or something comes along which helps to provide a needed solution. All of a sudden, we have an answer, a moment of relief, or help from someone we did not expect to receive, and it provides us with a renewed feeling of hope for our lives.

Do you believe those types of moments, when people come along at just the right time, are random events or were somehow pre-planned? Consider someone who has come into your life recently, a person you may still know to this date. How is it we are able to meet people and seemingly get along, as if we have known them our entire lives? Or how is possible that the right people come along at the right time, just when we need solutions to problems or challenges? The same is true for events which do not directly involve people, such as a check arriving in the mail.

Are these events random in nature, based upon luck, or given because a person was deemed worthy to receive assistance?

If you ask a group of people these questions, you are going to receive a wide variety of answers. Many of the answers are going to be related to prayers having been answered, and intervention from a supreme being or beings. If you believe in more non-traditional spiritual teachings, you might state the universe itself orchestrated people and events, or source has lined up the cooperative components for you. But what if there is something more involved to people coming in and out of our lives other than luck, involvement of a supreme being, intervention by the universe or source, or something else mystical in nature? Would you be willing to consider the possibility events in our lives have been already planned and nothing is occurring randomly or out of order?

I realize this goes against the idea of a supreme being acting as the one in control of the universe and all life; however, I have come to learn the true source of life is the energy of life we are all connected to, the Collective Consciousness of mankind. We, as humans, had to give this consciousness a name and this is how supreme being names were developed. But it is this consciousness which nurtures all of life and this is what we are all connected to at all times, and never cut off from no matter how bad we feel. Through this consciousness we are able to live as humans, and when we can free our mind of self-imposed limitations, we can access the Universal Wisdom of all of mankind. This is when we can discover universal laws and truths. We can also learn of the plan for our lives, which allows us to find our purpose and live a fulfilled and meaningful existence.

What all of this means to me is that there must be advanced plans developed while we are still in energetic form and deciding to come into a physical form. But what I wanted to know, while I focused my thoughts and attuned to Universal Wisdom, is how we (in energetic form) make arrangements with others for the timing of events here on Earth which feel to us (as humans) to be random, just in time, or just when needed. These pre-made arrangements are almost too complex for a rational, thinking, finite human mind to comprehend, yet I wanted to know what I could learn, and I will share with you what I was able to learn about the Law of Universal Agreements.

A universal truth is this: All is well in the universe. If you look above and see the sky, the planets, the stars, and the vast open space, you know there is an energy source sustaining all of this life, along with all of the living systems within it. There is order, and there is balance, even when it may seem at a micro level, or within certain areas on Planet Earth, that nothing but chaos exists.

Do You Feel a Sense of Hopelessness?

If you believe there is no hope left for this world, or the citizens of this Planet Earth, then take some time to unplug from all forms of technology first, to see how the removal of negative rhetoric begins to cause a seismic shift within your mind. Then take time to go to a place where you can experience a connection to nature, such as a mountain range, a rocky coastal shore, a desert oasis, or any place in nature where you can allow yourself to experience silence with yourself and without technology or other distractions. The purpose is to find stillness and become aware of nothing but nature around you.

When you can accomplish this task, you will begin to restore the inner peace you may have lost or shielded away as a result of the noise of everyday living. The universe is in order and it is mankind who creates disorder. To clarify, it is the Collective Consciousness of mankind, which is part of the energy of life, serving as the brain or operating system for the energy of life, keeping it functioning and in order.

As energetic beings come forward into physical forms as humans, it fulfills a specific purpose. Humans are designed or programmed for conflict as the tension creates both positive and negative energy. If energy could exist on positive energy alone, all humans would live in perfect harmony at all times. But the challenges, along with negative feelings, emotions, and conflicts, all lead to changes within humans. It may bring about new ideas and solutions, but most often wisdom is gained and this is how Universal Wisdom expands.

Awakening to a Truth About Life

One of the most amazing discoveries a human can make, as they begin to understand the order of the universe, is that their life was not random in nature or happened by accident. A person may never fully remember their energetic connection, or existence prior to coming into a physical form, yet they can awaken to a knowledge of a life being lived by a purpose and design.

For some, the initial thought of having a life already planned can be extremely frightening. There may be questions about choices made ahead of time, and why aspects of this life were brought about in the manner chosen. More importantly, it changes the nature of what was taught by religious institutions, who dictate man is controlled by a supreme being and there are laws which must be conformed to if benefits or assistance is to be received. Many humans are also taught their lives have been planned by this supreme being and to think otherwise creates a sense of having disobeyed something sacred. Changing a mindset from one that is controlled to one which takes control requires determination and strength.

This is why for other humans, an awakening to the truth about life can be freeing, as now a person may be able to let go of regret or holding onto past memories. Now a future focus can begin, or at the very least, the start of new goals may be possible. But knowledge of a life already planned also means a person can watch for clues as to how to fulfill this plan and ensure there are no delays in its coming to fruition. While a life plan may not change, the concept of free will does apply and this means a person can delay aspects of their plan by developing negative mental patterns or negative thoughts.

When a person becomes so attuned to the negative spectrum it becomes very difficult then to receive insight and wisdom from the Collective Consciousness. When a person is able to feel moments of happiness, love, hope, or anything else positive, they find themselves attuning to the positive spectrum.

Dreams Can Be Inspiring

One of the most inspirational sources of ideas and clues for a person's life plan is within their dreams. While many believe dreams hold clues about the lives of humans, which could be possible, dreams also provide future clues as a source of inspiration. There are no rules concerning dreams. Just as there is no supreme being dictating control of the universe, only a Collective Consciousness providing a source of direction for the life energy, there is no one dictating how dreams are to be used.

Dreams come from the subconsciousness mind, that which is connected directly to the Collective Consciousness. If a person believes they have relived events of the day, it was a strong emotional day and those emotions connected to the Collective Consciousness. It was an energy transfer experienced in the dreams. But a dream which seems unknown, exciting, uplifting, inspiring, hopeful, and full of vivid images, those are likely clues of the future. Those dreams usually stay with a person and repeat often.

Understanding Random Events

When humans then consider all of these vast and complex energetic processes, from how the mind operates to how the Collective Consciousness interacts with the minds of humans, it becomes easier to see there is a vast energetic network which exists. Somehow everything, which means every life, every mind, and every living thing, is all connected by this vast invisible energetic network.

Now consider this: The times when help comes along, just as you need it. Or you meet someone and it feels as if you have already known them, or there was an immediate connection as a soulmate. Is this just a matter of a person's mind tapping into the vast energetic network, asking for assistance and then receiving it?

Does a person ask for a mate, lover, or spouse and then one appears as promised by those who teach Law of Attraction? Why do people seem to suddenly appear in and out of our lives, almost as if they are random events? The answers to these questions involve more than Law of Attraction or random occurrences as it is part of the life plan this person has designed. While a person can think a thought, or think about a person and it seems the person will then appear, there is more involved.

The answer has to do with the Law of Universal Agreements.

Law of Universal Agreements

When an energetic form, which is a being or collective of pre-existing memories, is within the Collective Consciousness of mankind, and is deciding to come forward in physical form, a plan is made. A life plan is developed, from physical form birth, to physical form death or shedding the physical from the energy source.

The energetic being then scans the energetic network of the Collective Consciousness of mankind, examining the life plans stored; which are kept in the neutral area of the energy spectrums - or in between the positive and negative energy spectrums. The energetic being knows all of the outcomes, choices, and decisions to be made, for the physical form decided upon, along with the paths to be taken while here on Earth as a human being.

The energetic being sees points within the physical life when assistance is needed and by scanning other life plans, finds those who can provide the assistance. A universal agreement is reached so the life plans can intersect at some point. The specifics are further worked out, as to whether or not the meeting will be short-term or long-term. The meeting may be for help, friendship, a lover, boyfriend, girlfriend, mate, companion, husband, wife, or something else. The energetic being may leave some agreements as short-term and some as long-term, depending upon the need.

The life plan may have challenges and problems added in. Some may be left as a teaching or learning strategy, to prompt growth. Others may require help and the use of Universal Agreements. But all aspects of the life plan are evaluated as they are made, with every detail known. Then as part of the energetic being comes forward into the physical form, the mind of the physical form is nurtured by the energy, and the functions of the body run by the mind. But the mind will not immediately remember the internal connection to the Collective Consciousness - unless it was planned. What this writer is learning is this: He came forward remembering more than most people. This was his purpose. It would lead him to this point in time so he could learn to attune quickly and strongly.

You can also feel your connection to the Collective Consciousness of mankind. First, believe in your ability to live the life you want. What you feel deep inside is the blueprint for the life you have already created, calling out to you. Next, listen or pay attention to your dreams. Feel the images you see as you dream or as you think about your ideal future. What moves you? What excites you? Then, pay attention to the people who come into your life. Even this teacher is serving a purpose to help you now.

You can have the life you have planned. Clear your mind of doubt because there is no reason not to believe. Watch for the clues and see how life unfolds for you. Trust you have access to unlimited insight and wisdom, and in time you will believe it, as the limiting beliefs you hold are released.

Who Is Controlling the Universe?

If you stop to consider how the planets are operating within the vast solar system, and then how life is sustained here on planet Earth, it would seem to our human, logical mind that this has all been planned out and then carefully managed. But the question most people would ask is this: Who has planned it and who is managing it? Who is in control of the universe and all of life?

Most people would respond quickly and state that God, or some other supreme being, is the one who is in control and dictates the order of the universe and even our lives, based upon a master plan. Those who follow Law of Attraction teachers may simply state the universe is in control, or source is controlling people and events. In other words, some divine being or higher power is responsible for determining how all of our lives are planned and how the world evolves. And most people seem to be content with this way of thinking as it is handed down from one generation to the next.

In religious institutions, there is a sacred book which remains unchanged to this day and is the resource that provides the evidence of who is controlling the universe. This again is accepted by followers, even if the basis of the sacred book could be easily called into question for its lack of credibility and authenticity, with regard to how it was put together, how it was edited, the purpose for which it was put together, and its lack of relevance for today's people. People still to this day believe it is the final authority and they also willingly accept someone else is above and below them in mythical existences, either exerting control or attempting to influence them for their evil purposes.

But as a teacher of the Laws of the Universe, I have come to learn new truths about the order of our lives, the universe, and even our very existence. I know about the nature of the source of life energy, yet I still have questions about the involvement of this life energy in the development of the plans for each of our lives. I want to know how actively involved this energy of life source is when it comes to managing the universe and all of life. I wanted to see if I could gain clarity while connected to Collective Consciousness about the issue of control and answer the question: Who is controlling the universe? I will share with you what I have learned.

A universal truth is this: Mankind has a consciously finite ability to think, and a subconscious infinite ability to vibrate or attune. The finite conscious ability to think means that man must rationalize, analyze, consider, weight, evaluate, and work through information being processed in the mind. At a conscious level, man cannot consider a life without control of any form as it defies the logical or rational thinking. Of course, some humans can train themselves to become less conscious oriented, which means they become more subconscious or intuitive oriented, allowing their thinking to originate not from the rational or logical mind but from the subconscious fully attuned mind.

The subconscious fully attuned mind is connected to the Collective Consciousness and higher order Universal Wisdom. Someone who is called intuitive has become less logical or rational minded and more focused on receiving wisdom from Collective Consciousness. This writer is receiving direct wisdom from Universal Wisdom now through a practiced habit of turning off the rational mind, and just allowing wisdom to flow through without any reservations, hesitation, bias, or filters.

While in this attuned state of mind, it is possible to think of the universe just functioning on its own and without any direct help. But the logical or rational mind, with its finite limitations, must have a reason for the existence and ongoing operation of the universe.

Control of the Universe

There is no need to control the universe because every element of the universe is related to energy. The source of life energy is the energy which is nurtured by mankind and in turn nurtured by all of life. There is an unending cycle of new physical life coming forward, the energy nurturing Collective Consciousness and causing it to expand, and physical forms being shed. It is a perpetual cycle. Each person in energetic form decides their physical form prior to arrival, and all components of the plan are aligned. The plan happens not because someone is in control, but because humans are in control.

The universe needs no control as it is perpetually sustained and nurtured, never running out of life or energy. Humans begin as energy, make plans, make arrangements for those plans, and then extend their energy into part physical and part energetic forms. There is no supreme being or higher power in control. All humans, or all of mankind, have contributed to the sustenance of the universe in some manner. The idea of control is only a human one. Only humans think in terms of control. The universe exists as it is, without needing help or assistance. It is supported and nurtured by the energy of life, which is all around and within all living things.

Man's View of the Universe

The idea of a universe not needing to be controlled can be quite chaotic for many humans. It would seem that could not possibly be or else the entire planetary system as we know it would be in sheer chaos. More importantly, if no one is in control of the universe, who do humans turn to when they need help with their lives? How can they find answers to important questions? Who do they pray to during dark times or times which are exceedingly challenging?

Those who can switch to a more intuitive or open mind will discover they have an ability to be in control of their lives. They can attune, look for clues about the plan for their lives, and no longer need to seek help from someone else or a higher power.

Humans want to know about order in the universe when they are taught to depend upon a supreme being, but they find their lives are not going well and they feel nothing but a sense of helplessness. That loss of control feels so bad it would seem there is no way possible the universe could be run this way. But the bad feeling of being helpless is really not about control of the universe, it's about being dependent upon someone else to create your life. The truth is that only you have the power to create your life's plan. If you are seeking answers about life, you will need to learn to look within first.

What this means is going beyond the logical or rational mind. Or first applying the logical and rational mind to the information you have accepted as truths all of your life. Ask yourself about the supreme being you have been told who runs the universe. Can this possibly be true? Ask yourself why you have accepted so many religious teachings as truths without stopping to consider if these were in fact truths.

Once you can begin to question what you hold to be truths, you can then begin to allow yourself to turn within to seek answers. Instead of looking outward or to someone else to help you with your life, you will look for ways to solve the problems, issues, and challenges you are facing by listening for the insight and wisdom you have access to at any time. When you can accept that you are connected to the source of life, and have access to the wisdom of mankind, your life will begin to change. You will not need to look for someone else in charge. The universe is you; living, breathing, energy.

CHAPTER 7.
HOW TO GUIDE

There are three typical questions which may arise while reading this book and include:

How do I best use this book?

There are many laws of the universe, how do I use them?

How do I create a personal and spiritual transformation?

What you will find is that you transform as you learn about who you are, the purpose of your life, and the plan you have created for your life. You accomplish this goal as you discover your belief systems and underlying view of life.

You can use this book as part of a weekly commitment or plan for personal self-development. As you learn about yourself, you will see or discover how Laws of the Universe manage life and are a foundation for transformation in your life.

What follows is a plan for use of this book by reading it according to the topic of interest each week, with a related chapter and subheading provided for each suggested topic.

Discover How to Bring About Your Transformation

Below is a list of topics you can choose from each week based upon your own interests.

Topic: What Do I Believe About Religion

Read: Chapter 2. EVERYTHING IS ENERGY

What Are Names Associated with Energy?

Is Energy the Same as God or a Supreme Being?

Topic: What Do I Believe About the Universe?
Read: Chapter 6. READ AND BELIEVE
Who Is Controlling the Universe?

Topic: What Do I Know About Energy?
Read: Chapter 2. EVERYTHING IS ENERGY
What is Energy?
What is the Mind and Body Connection?
What Are the Different Forms of Energy?

Topic: What is the Source of Life?
Read: Chapter 3. COLLECTIVE CONSCIOUSNESS
The Energy Source of Life
Our Connection to Collective Consciousness

Topic: Have I Learned to Accept Myself?
Read: Chapter 1. ONE MAN'S TRANSFORMATIONAL JOURNEY
Discovering Self-Acceptance

Topic: Why is My Life So Different?
Read: Chapter 1. ONE MAN'S TRANSFORMATIONAL JOURNEY
Why Would Someone Choose to Live a Unique Life?

Topic: How Do I Stay Focused on the Present?
Read: Chapter 3. COLLECTIVE CONSCIOUSNESS
Live Your Current Reality

Topic: How Do I Keep Positive When Life is Bleak?
Read: Chapter 5. THE IMPORTANCE OF YOUR MINDSET
How Do You Keep a Positive Outlook About Life?

Topic: How Do I Keep from Feeling Overwhelmed?
Read: Chapter 5. THE IMPORTANCE OF YOUR MINDSET
How to Find Relief from Feeling Overwhelmed

Topic: How Do I Manage Change?
Read: Chapter 5. THE IMPORTANCE OF YOUR MINDSET
Understand the Energy of Change

Topic: What Important Questions Do I Have Now?
Read: Chapter 5. THE IMPORTANCE OF YOUR MINDSET
How Do You Find Answers to Important Questions?

Topic: Can I Learn to Reflect and Find Insight?
Read: Chapter 5. THE IMPORTANCE OF YOUR MINDSET
How to Tap into and Benefit from Universal Wisdom

Topic: Do I Feel a Sense of Self-Worth?
Read: Chapter 6. READ AND BELIEVE
How Do You Learn Self-Worth?

Topic: What Do I Believe About Abundance?
Read: Chapter 6. READ AND BELIEVE
How Do You Find Abundance?

Topic: Who Created My Life's Plan?
Read: Chapter 6. READ AND BELIEVE
Can Someone Amend Their Life's Plan?

Topic: Are Events in Life Random?
Read: Chapter 6. READ AND BELIEVE
What are Random Events?

Topic: Do I Need to Show Gratitude?
Read: Chapter 5. THE IMPORTANCE OF YOUR MINDSET
What Is the Higher Purpose of Gratitude?

Topic: Are Relationships Permanent?
Read: Chapter 4. LAWS OF THE UNIVERSE
Law of Connection: Forming Attachments

Topic: What Do I Believe About Vibrations?
Read: Chapter 4. LAWS OF THE UNIVERSE
Law of Attunement: Changing Your Focus and Vibration

Topic: Can I Influence How I Interact with Others?
Read: Chapter 4. LAWS OF THE UNIVERSE
Law of Interaction: Internal and External Interactions

Topic: Who Created the Life I'm Living?
Read: Chapter 4. LAWS OF THE UNIVERSE
Law of Intention: Creating Your Own Life

Topic: How Do I Find My Purpose?

Read: Chapter 4. LAWS OF THE UNIVERSE

Law of Presence: Fulfilling Your Purpose

Topic: How Do I Process Grief?

Read: Chapter 4. LAWS OF THE UNIVERSE

The Law of the Duality of Energy: Experiencing Negative Emotions

Topic: How Do I Deal with Challenges?

Read: Chapter 4. LAWS OF THE UNIVERSE

Law of Clarity: Understanding the Purpose of Challenges

Printed in Great Britain
by Amazon